Experiencing His Presence

Devotions for God Catchers

TOMMY TENNEY

THOMAS NELSON PUBLISHERS®

A Division of Thomas Nelson Publishing, Inc.
www.ThomasNelson.com

*This book is dedicated to my faithful and incredible editor, Larry Walker.
Much of what you read in this book would be but uncut diamonds without his
expertise. They would appear to be just another sequence of unremarkable
rocks in the pathway of life. Larry has a unique ability to capture concepts in
their rough form, reveal their every facet, and polish them to reveal their true
qualities as brilliant diamonds reflecting the light of the Son.*

Copyright © 2001 by Tommy Tenney

Published in Nashville, Tennessee, by Thomas Nelson, Inc.

Unless otherwise noted, Scripture quotations are from THE NEW KING JAMES VERSION. Copyright © 1979, 1980,
1982 by Thomas Nelson, Inc. Used by permission. All rights reserved.

Scripture quotations noted KJV are from the KING JAMES VERSION.

Tenney, Tommy, 1956–
　　　Experiencing His presence: devotions for God catchers / Tommy Tenney.
　　　　　p. cm.
　　　ISBN 0-7852-6619-4
　　　　1. Spiritual Life—Christianity. 2. Prayer books and devotions. I. Tenney, Tommy. II. Title.
　　　BV4501.3 .T455 2001
　　　242'.2—dc21　　　　　　　　　　　　　　　　　　　　　　　　　　　　　2001044825
　　　　　　　　　　　　　　　　　　　　　　　　　　　　　　　　　　　　　CIP

Printed in the United States of America

01 02 03 04 05 BVG 5 4 3 2 1

Contents

Notes for the Chase from a Fellow Chaser

Before we begin our devotional pursuit of His presence, you should know that I developed this devotional with several basic assumptions in mind.

First, I assume that you *want* to pursue God's face, and that you don't feel compelled to do it for all of the wrong reasons.

Second, I *assume* that you have some basic elements of discipleship in your life, such as a personal prayer life and daily times of intimacy with God. If you do not, then this is a good time to strengthen these areas.

A God Chaser without these basic elements of the Christian life is like a race car chassis and body without an engine, transmission, fuel system, or steering mechanism. He has all of the characteristics of an empty religious shell going nowhere fast. In fact, if you are not a God Chaser, you can never be a God Catcher.

Third, I assume that you will bring a well-used Bible with you for the chase. Any book such as this written by a human author should be considered only a tool or a road sign leading you deeper into God's Book, or encouraging you to pick up the pace of your chase after the Divine Author who penned it through anointed men. If you are a new Bible student, I encourage you to look up every Bible reference mentioned in *Experiencing His Presence*. The Scriptures are the deep well from which true revelation flows.

The true God Chaser loves and devours God's Word. I preach it, teach it, proclaim it, memorize it, study it, meditate on it, and extensively quote it in some form every single day and in every message I share. By now you know how strongly I feel that you should make God's Word part of your daily spiritual diet as a God Chaser.

Fourth, since God is "An Equal Opportunity Redeemer" who wants to see everyone saved,[1] I assume that you know that God allows Himself to be "caught" by Roman Catholic and Orthodox chasers just as quickly as He turns to pursue passionate Baptist, Methodist, Episcopalian, Presbyterian, charismatic, or Pentecostal pursuers. (He also has a habit of dropping in on passionate Jewish pursuers from time to time. Just ask Paul the apostle.)

He is equally unimpressed whether we boast in our denominational ties or tout our independence from organized Christian church groups—as far as He is concerned, there is only *one church* gathered under a single blood-red banner emblazoned with the name of His Son, Jesus Christ.

I've seen His presence suddenly descend on God Chasers in high church services, folk masses, high-energy contemporary worship services, and intimate prayer times with an audience of One. Jesus is the Door, and broken worship is His favorite fragrance—whether the broken vessel at His feet is of Baptist, Christian Church, Mennonite, Nazarene, United Brethren, or Reformed "alabaster."

Fifth, I assume that your goal is to pursue *God* throughout this devotional journey (not simply the limited thoughts of this thoroughly human author). I embrace the desire of John the Baptist who said, "He must increase, but I must decrease."[2] My fervent prayer is that with each step you take in the chase, His voice will grow stronger and my voice will grow weaker. In the end may we all say, "It's not about us; it's all about *Him*."

Finally, I assume that some may choose to bring some friends into the chase in the form of a Bible study group or a Sunday school class, or simply use this devotional as a discipleship tool to help draw a younger Christian into the chase of a lifetime. For this reason, you will find that the questions and insights developed in this book are easily adapted for use in group study, interpersonal interaction, and corporate prayer.

Even if you go through this devotional in a group setting of some kind, I encourage you to spend time alone with God each day. Take this personal devotional and your Bible with you, and seek out a private place where you won't be disturbed. And don't forget a personal journal and a pen or pencil so you can keep a record of the things the Holy Spirit reveals to you along the way.

When you come across a question in the devotional, don't rush past it to "finish the assignment." Your only assignment is to *experience His presence*, not just come up with an answer. The questions I pose should help you prepare your heart and mind for the chase. Beyond that, the results of your God Chase depend mostly on the depth of your desire and the passion of your pursuit.

It is possible that if you seek Him diligently and long for Him with all of your being, then you will be "found" by Him. I remember reading somewhere that we should "seek the LORD while He may be found."[3]

The greatest blessings of God's Word come to those who are *doers* of His Word. The chase is on. If our passion is hot and our worship sweet, then we who pursue Him may yet become God Catchers by grace, the pursued of God truly *experiencing His presence*.

> Your partner in the pursuit
> of His presence,
> *Tommy Tenney*

Does God Play Hide-and-Seek?

*Things I Wish I Knew the Day
I Nearly Caught Him*

Launched on a journey "of His own choosing," you find yourself hungry, thirsty, passionate, and adrift on the sea of divine grace.

God's Word is your navigational chart, divine discontent your compass, and the bread of His presence your chief desire.

Does God play hide-and-seek, or is it that He simply doesn't care? The truth may be sweeter than you know and more costly than you ever dreamed.

Does Hunger Bring God Out of Hiding?

Your favorite services and My favorite services are not the same. You leave your services full and satisfied, but when you leave, I'm still hungry.

THE GOD CATCHERS, P. 2

SCRIPTURE READING:

Psalm 84, where we discover the blessings to be found in God's courts when heart and flesh cry out for Him.

Divine interruptions in our daily affairs provide some of our most significant "proofs" of God's existence. In one moment, perhaps just half a moment, the God beyond time can invade our clock-driven existence and turn our world upside down.

Have you ever experienced a divine interruption? How did you respond to it? Was it a brief interruption for the moment, or a divine marker signaling a lifelong course change?

As I noted in *The God Catchers*, God "interrupted my self-defined successful career as a full-time evangelist with a simple but shocking revelation: *You know, Tommy, your favorite services and My favorite services are not the same. You leave your services full and satisfied, but when you leave, I'm still hungry*" (p. 2).

That brief statement suddenly reduced two and a half decades of ministry to a frustrated journey from God's good to God's best. A sick feeling engulfed me when I realized that much of what I had been doing as a well-intentioned full-time evangelist may have helped to perpetuate the kind of services that left God hungry and dissatisfied.

I left that God encounter with a permanent spiritual limp, knowing I could never again support or be satisfied by "church as usual." You may not be a full-time minister, but you do play a role through your worship and ministry to the Lord in every service.

Have you experienced something similar to what I did? What can you do to make sure God leaves your church service satisfied instead of hungry?

The Lord began to teach me about the importance of being a God Chaser during a nine-month period of what I call "divine discontent," when I learned that the only way we can bless God in our meetings is to leave them feeling hungrier for Him than when we first came.

How would you describe your hunger level and the way you feel about it right now?

The term *divine discontent* is described this way in my first book, *The God Chasers*:

I somehow sensed that destiny was waiting . . . a hunger had been birthed in my heart that just wouldn't go away. The gnawing vacuum of emptiness in the midst of my accomplishments just got worse. I was in a frustrating funk, a divine depression of destiny . . . I just sensed that something awaited us from God.[1]

My personal season of divine discontent ultimately led to an encounter with God that turned my life upside down and permanently rearranged my ministry. As of this writing, I haven't "recovered," and I pray that I never do!

Can you identify with the term *divine discontent*? Are you ready for a life-changing God encounter?

Prayer

I'm ready, Lord. I've waited and pretended too long. The divine discontent in my soul is unbearable, and my hunger for more of You is a consuming fire. Finish Your work in me, Lord, and in my pursuit of Your presence let me become the pursued.

True Confessions of a God Addict

Now I am no longer content just to "chase" Him. I want to "catch" Him, to collect a string of close encounters with Him. Sometimes I grow weary with the daily chase, but I must chase if I want to catch.

THE GOD CATCHERS, P. 3

SCRIPTURE READING:

Psalm 27:4, in which David reveals the deepest desire of his heart—to "dwell in the house of the Lord" all the days of his life and behold His beauty.

The natural world contains countless hints about the absolute addictive nature of intimacy with Divinity. It is said that crack cocaine is so addictive that many who decide to try it just once find themselves irresistibly drawn into its wicked web of ever-growing addiction and compulsive drive for more.

The list of overwhelming compulsions preying on us seems to grow longer by the month. Some people grow compulsively addicted to gambling, ever chasing one final throw of the dice or the extra set of lottery tickets that will land them a jackpot so large it will forever solve their financial woes.

For others, their virtually uncontrollable compulsions lean more toward the buffet line, the dessert tray, or the hotel bars and liquor stores. More than a few fall into the darkness of sensual addictions too awful to imagine or describe.

How can such things so far removed from God be considered hints about some kind of God addiction? The answer concerns the very fact that our race has such a capacity for unfulfilled desire, and has nothing to do with the things for which human beings become addicted.

Have you noticed that capacity for unbridled desire in your life? Is it so strong that you fear you would throw away everything for one more taste, for just one more touch of what seems unattainable? If this desire burns for anything or anyone other than God, beware. If your passion is turned God-ward, why fight it?

I am convinced that God put this infinite capacity for addiction in our hearts, and that its only cure and true satisfaction is found in the infinite riches of the presence of the One who loves us with limitless love. He is, in essence, the only legal addiction for our race in the created universe (and there is no *compulsion* in this addiction).

Does it feel strange to speak of an "addiction" for God? Maybe you've been taught that addiction in any form is wrong and a sign of weakness or a disability. Are you willing to be called a weak or disabled person because you pursue Him with incurable passion?

C. S. Lewis, the celebrated Cambridge professor, thinker, and brilliant defender of the Christian faith, wrote in *The Problem of Pain*:

The mould in which a key is made would be a strange thing, if you had never seen a key: and the key itself a strange thing if you had never seen a lock. Your soul has a curious shape because it is a hollow made to fit a particular swelling in the infinite contours of the divine substance, or a key to unlock one of the doors in the house with many mansions . . .

. . . Blessed and fortunate creature, your eyes shall behold Him and not another's. All that you are, sins apart, is destined, if you will let God have His good way, to utter satisfaction . . . God will look to every soul like its first love because *He is* its first love.[2]

I must confess that I am an incurable addict, hopelessly seeking an eternal fix for the unending longing within me. I long to see Him as He is in all of His glory. *What about you?*

Prayer

Dear Lord, one taste of perfection is not enough. Even the hint of Your nearness sparks unspeakable longing for more. I confess that I am weak, disabled, ineffective, and lost without You. You are the Water for which I thirst, the Bread for which I hunger. You are my Hope, my Joy, and my Chief Desire.

THE THIRD DAY

Early Hints of Passionate Perfume

Even then I had hints in my heart that, in some supernatural way, the pursuer becomes the pursued when God catches wind of our worship and praise.

THE GOD CATCHERS, P. 4

SCRIPTURE READING:

Psalm 22:3, where God's throne is defined and described.

Perhaps you've experienced the "suddenly" of His unexpected arrival in a meeting, in your car, or in the wee hours of the morning. His presence didn't linger the first time; it captivated you and then evaporated too soon.

How long ago did those first hints of something holy and heavenly first touch your life? What did you do about it? Did you pursue it, seeking more? What happened? Did you forget it after a while and resume the "normal" things that fill your life?

The pursuit of God's presence may earn you criticism and scorn at times, especially from the friends and enemies who talk about "walking by faith and not by sight."[3] They are right about living by faith, but they are wrong if they interpret that Bible phrase to mean we should live by theology and not by experience, and by mental assent and not by personal relationship.

If God didn't exist, perhaps a passionless existence would be acceptable. But He does exist, and because He lives, we can live. Since the Bible is a true witness, then the God we serve is a God of infinite passion and delight, and He could never be classified as a mere divine law clerk keeping score solely for the sake of eternal judgment. Judgment Day will surely come, but God's greatest focus is on a passionate wedding and the riotous celebration that will mark its consummation.

None of this can ever be "argued" into you. It usually comes straight to the heart—unannounced and unexpected. Like an arrow of heaven, just enough of His love and delight pierces your soul to drive a thrill (yes, I said *thrill!*) through every cell of your body. If the physical thrill was all we longed for, then we could find solace in the needle, pill, and/or bottle. Yet these will not do. We are after Him.

The faith comes in during those times when there is more pursuing than catching. Yet God never intended for us to make a religion out of being unrequited lovers and lousy losers who never quite connect with the heart of God. That just doesn't match up with the same God who so loved the world that He gave His only begotten Son!

As I wrote in *The God Catchers,*

I've learned more about the fuel of desperation and the feel of destiny while in pursuit of His presence. The Lord also taught me more about embracing this place of what I previously called a "frustrating funk, a divine depression of destiny." Weariness with man can birth desperation for God. (p. 4)

Do you find it strange that in the middle of all the crises and difficulties in the Bible we so often find praise and worship? When trouble invades your life, what is your first instinct? Do you gripe and complain at Him or worship and praise Him?

Paul and Silas worshiped Him from their jail cell. Paul worshiped Him throughout a lifetime of suffering and hardship. David wrote some of his most exalted psalms from the dismal interior of the cave Adullam in exile from his own nation, family, and home. Perhaps we should find it even stranger that praise and worship are so often *absent* from our daily lives.

PRAYER

Lord, You've supplied hints of "more" all of my life. Today I say, "Here I am, Lord. I am Yours." I will worship and praise You, no matter how I feel or how great the adversity facing me. I'm confident that once You catch wind of my worship and desperate need for You, You will come.

His Hiding Has More to Do with Joy than with Judgment

At least eleven times in the Psalms, David said in effect, "You are a God who hides Himself . . ." Why would the God of the universe, the almighty Creator, hide Himself from His creation? . . . I think the biblical answer has more to do with joy than with judgment.

THE GOD CATCHERS, P. 6

SCRIPTURE READING:

Daniel 10:12, when the angel of God appears to Daniel and says he has been sent "because of your words."

To those who don't pursue Him, God seems to be hiding all of the time. To God Chasers like King David who become obsessed with the pursuit of His presence, even a moment of hiding or separation can seem like an eternity.

Where do you fit in this picture? Do you feel that God is more or less permanently hidden from you, or are you growing more and more obsessed with the pursuit of His presence because you are convinced He allows Himself to be caught?

The common understanding in David's day (and in ours as well, for that matter) is that God hid Himself from men and women so His holiness wouldn't destroy them in their sin. There is definitely truth to that understanding, but God Chasers don't fear judgment as much as they fear separation from their Beloved.

Long before Jesus shed His atoning blood on the cross, God permitted David to break all the rigid rules of the priesthood and of the Most Holy Place. David used to take his favorite footstool to the tent on Mount Zion and sit right in front of the ark of the covenant just so he could be near the presence of God.[4]

How often do you retreat to your favorite "footstool" to sit before the Lord in sweet communion? Is it often enough?

On page 6 of *The God Catchers,* I said,

Why would the God of the universe, the almighty Creator, hide Himself from His creation? We know, for instance, that He hides Himself from sin and pride, basically because He doesn't want His absolute holiness to destroy us in our pollution. But that isn't the main reason that God hides. He sent His only Son to take care of the sin problem forever once we repent and turn to Him.

I read somewhere that it was "for the joy that was set before Him" that Jesus endured the cross, scorned the shame, and took His seat at the right hand of the throne of God.[5] The judgment of sin was clearly involved in Jesus' journey to the cross, but it seems that joy, not judgment, *propelled* Him through the unspeakable sorrow of the grave to the exultation of resurrection morning.

What motivates or empowers your Christian walk the most? The critical judgment of other people or the joy of discovery in His presence?

In the same way, I'm convinced the joy of discovery prompts God to "hide" from us at times (and these are the moments we remember best). Sometimes during a meeting I will ask who remembers the topic of the sermon delivered on the day they first received Christ as Savior and sensed the first glimmer of His presence in their hearts. At best, I usually see only a few hands go up. Then I ask how many people remember the *experience* they had the time they first discovered the Savior who loves them. Without exception, the meeting places take on the appearance of a sea of waving hands. Why?

How would you respond to these questions? What stands out the most in your personal history with God? Your failures or His triumphs?

It isn't a concept that saves us; it is Jesus Christ. We don't merely embrace and dedicate the rest of our lives to a theology about God; we embrace *Him* who first loved us.[6] This is generally our first taste of what happens when the pursuer suddenly becomes the pursued of God.

PRAYER

Lord, we know You hide from us for many reasons. My greatest encouragement doesn't come from Your hiding; it springs from Your sudden appearing in my moments of deep need or searing hunger for Your companionship. I will be eternally hungry for You if it means You will meet me again.

When Sunday Morning Kisses Aren't Enough

God doesn't leave . . . He lingers. His greatest joy is to extend and expand the moments of encounter. Sunday morning kisses are not enough!

THE GOD CATCHERS, PP. 7–8

SCRIPTURE READING:

Isaiah 29:13, in which God indicts Israel because the people honored Him with their lips but not their hearts. Their worship was rooted only in rules made up by men.

Do you ever have the sinking feeling that what we do in church could continue just as well whether or not God ever showed up? I fear that we have so formalized our relationship with God that all He receives from us in the brief times we gather in His name is lip service, those fluttery fake kisses we usually reserve for strangers on formal occasions. We also give fake kisses to people or relatives we barely know and really don't care to know better.

Have you ever given God a fake kiss on Sunday morning so you could do what you wanted to do on Sunday afternoon?

The problem with fake kisses is that they carry no commitment or obligation with them. Passionate kisses may lead to something deeper, something more costly and more involved than we are prepared for.

There is no deeper commitment than the eternal covenant we make with God the day we receive His forgiveness and enter an eternal relationship of

14

intimacy with Divinity. Yet we insist on giving Him brief, controlled kisses during our rigid and schedule-driven meetings each week. He must feel more like a much-avoided aunt or an unappreciated neighbor than our Divine Groom and Redeemer. Nevertheless, He keeps pursuing us in the hope that one day our passion will rise and we will begin to pursue Him.

On page 12 of *The God Catchers,* I noted one simple and straightforward focus to keep: *how you can capture God's heart.* For a growing number of passionate pursuers around the world, that has also become the defining focus of their lives.

Are you one of "them"? Are you desperate for another encounter with Him? What keeps you in the chase—love or legalism? Distant and infrequent flirtations once a week, or passionate pursuit every waking moment?

Sunday morning kisses aren't enough for the God who ceaselessly searches for worshipers who will worship Him in spirit and in truth.[7] He is wondering when we will finally catch on and join in the joyful chase. He anticipates the day we make the joyful transition in our hearts from being simply the redeemed of the Lord to becoming the *betrothed* of the Lord, the bride of Christ, without spot or wrinkle. What is impossible for man and man's ways is entirely possible for God—when we yield to His way.

PRAYER

Lord, please forgive me for all of the fake kisses I've tossed to You on my way out the door of relationship and intimacy. Forgive me, I ask, for the times I've blindly sacrificed a lingering moment with You on the altar of my hurried schedule, of my order of service, or of my temporary human need for things and activities. Now I offer myself on the altar of my will as a living sacrifice. May I be pleasing to You.

On the Trail of True Passion:
Tracking Down Worshipers

At the very moment my little daughter would say, "Oh, Daddy," I would turn and begin to chase her. Worship turns the tables on the chase. It takes you to the point where you don't have to pursue Him because He begins to pursue you. If you are a worshiper, God will track you down.

THE GOD CATCHERS, P. 9

SCRIPTURE READING:

John 4:23, where Jesus upends the theological applecart of the ages to announce God's great passion; He scours the earth for true worshipers who worship Him in spirit and in truth.

Countless books, play scripts, screenplays, and dramatizations have portrayed various professional soldiers, adventurers, and leaders as unwilling to cultivate long-term relationships with spouses and family simply because they felt such interactions made them *vulnerable*. "If you have someone or something that you love greatly," the theory goes, "you give your enemies the ability to hurt you greatly by robbing you of your beloved."

Have you ever caught yourself holding something back from God while thinking, *What if He really isn't listening? What if He doesn't care?* Are you really willing to invest so much love in an invisible God you can't see?

It is no accident that soldiers over the centuries required their loved ones to stay home and as far away as possible from the field of battle. They would rather suffer hurt or even death than see their loved ones endangered.

God dares to love much, even though it exposes the Almighty to the pain of rejection and the possibility of theft (the theft of affections) by the deceiver of men. As long as men saw God primarily as a Celestial Judge who favored the administration of judgment over the distribution of grace, it appeared that God was risking very little. Then came the Cross, when heaven's Soldier literally laid down His life for His beloved. What do we do now?

Many people grew up thinking God was up in heaven with a baseball bat, ready to smack anyone who stepped out of line.

Were you one of them? What happened the first time you realized the truth about what Jesus did on the cross?

God has laid bare His passion for worshipers, and the truth is out for all to see. We have no excuse for clinging to our passionless religious ritual when we know our Maker desires and seeks *more* from us.

How much of the typical worship service really involves worship in spirit and in truth? What part of the service do you think would actually attract God's attention and cause Him to hunt you down?

At the bidding of the Father, Jesus risked everything for you and me. Now it is in our laps. Will we begin the passionate game of pursuit and capture again? The great Pursuer of worshipers is waiting for us to begin our song of praise and release passionate waves of worship and adoration toward His throne.

Allow me to paint a picture by rewriting a brief passage from *The God Catchers*. I've redirected the text from my relationship with my daughter to mirror God's relationship with the church:

And so the game began again. She was determined to kiss Me, but it wasn't hard for Me to avoid her. I could easily move this way and that way to dodge her— the created universe is but a finite playground for My infinity.

Within a few minutes, she usually gets tired and says, "Oh, Daddy," and stops her pursuit. She couldn't capture Me physically, but she easily captured Me emotionally. She couldn't move her religious services and self-made methods fast enough to apprehend Me, but her words easily captured My heart.[8]

Does anything in these two paragraphs touch your heart? Are you moved to change something in your life or worship to help you capture His heart?

PRAYER

In my weakness, Lord, I nearly gave up. I'm too slow to overtake You, too weak to keep up with You, and too limited in intellect to outsmart You. It is foolish for me to call myself a God Chaser unless You allow me to catch You.

I worship You. I love You. I desperately need You. You alone can satisfy the burning in my heart, O Daddy.

God Will Take a Trip in Time
Just to Be with You

God doesn't hide Himself from you so that He can't be found; He hides Himself from you so that He can be found. He hides for the sheer joy of being discovered.

THE GOD CATCHERS, P. 11

SCRIPTURE READING:

Revelation 3:20, where God issues the invitation of the ages to a weak and wandering church: "Behold, I stand at the door and knock. If anyone hears My voice and opens the door, I will come in to him and dine with him, and he with Me."

As a proud father, I consider it no sacrifice to endure a full day of inconvenience, fatigue, rushing crowds, and tightly packed aircraft just to "experience thirty seconds of my daughter's joy in the driveway."[9] No matter how hard or inconvenient it may be, it is *worth it to me* to see the joy of discovery in my daughter's eyes once again.

My experiences with my three beautiful daughters combined with the convincing testimony of the Scriptures led me to write in *The God Catchers*, "God will take a trip in time just to spend a brief moment with humanity. He thinks it's worth it to be with you!"[10]

Has it ever occurred to you that God really wants to be with you (as odd as that may seem)? Now that you know, has that concept changed anything in your thinking or lifestyle?

In *The God Catchers,* I noted that as my children grew older, they altered the way they related to me. One incident I experienced with my youngest daughter seemed to typify the reaction of the time-sensitive church when our heavenly Father wants "more love than we have time" to give Him:

Even though my youngest daughter has partially outgrown the hidey-face game, I can still manage to squeeze some great kisses and hugs from her if I really work at it. The other day I said, "Honey, come up here and give Daddy some love. Give me some kisses."

She was busy playing with some of her dolls and things, but she obediently crawled up on my lap and gave me a kiss. Then she was ready to get down again.

"No, come on. Give me some more love," I said.

Then she said, "That's the problem with you daddies."

"What do you mean?" I said.

"You always want too much love," she said.

I could only grin and say, "Yeah, I'm guilty."

That's the problem with our Daddy too: He always wants too much love. We give Him a perfunctory kiss on Sunday morning and hurry to return to our religious toys and pretend encounters. All the while He is saying, "I've been missing you; I'd love to have some more loving kisses and hugs from you."[11]

Do you agree with my statement "We've become more time sensitive than Spirit sensitive"?[12] Does this problem plague your personal relationship with God? What will you do about it?

PRAYER

Dear Lord, I used to pursue You for all of the wonderful things I found in Your hands. I loved to ask You for all of the things You've promised to me, but now I want more. I'm not hungry for more things, more thrills, or more favor with people. I just want You. I promise I'll lay aside my watches, schedules, programs, and habits if You will just come once again.

Burning Lips and Hot Hearts

Somebody Caught Him: The True Story of a God Catcher

Is it any surprise that Isaiah's first words to the Lord when he "caught" Him in the temple were, "Woe is me, for I am undone! Because I am a man of unclean lips"?[1] Even godly people feel ungodly in the manifest presence of the living God.

It took only one touch from the embers of God to give Isaiah burning lips and a heart so hot that, according to tradition, only martyrdom managed to silence his human voice (his prophetic message still thunders across the ages).

In our generation, nearly two millennia after the Cross, repentance is the new covenant equivalent of the old covenant sin offering, and the first step to a new beginning in Christ.

It takes only one encounter.

The Restless Remnant:
Incurably Desperate for a God Encounter

The restless remnant is comprised of "the few, the humble, and the broken" who refuse to bow their knees to false gods, false messiahs, false shepherds, or trivial religious pursuits because they want only to see His face and dwell in His presence. The big problem with this remnant is that its members aren't easily cataloged, cross-referenced, or "boxed." Their only common characteristic (and the only prerequisite for membership) is their defining hunger for the presence of the living God.

THE GOD CATCHERS, PP. 193–94

SCRIPTURE READING:

John 4:24, where Jesus describes the worship of the restless remnant God seeks.

Most people do everything they can to avoid labels, stereotypes, and social tags. The most popular and effective avoidance technique may be compromise. If you choose to be a true God Chaser, and especially if you become a God Catcher; are you willing to be labeled as "incurably desperate" and "addicted"?

God finds it difficult or impossible to work with those who are desperate for the approval of people; but He can move mountains, nations, and entire generations with men, women, and children who are incurably desperate for Him.

It all seems to begin with the cry God can't deny, the urgent cry of a desperate heart longing for His divine touch. If you've had your fill of "religious stage gymnastics and emotional hype designed to excite and stroke the flesh," and if you are "sick of church games, man's manipulation, and passionless worship," then you need an encounter with the Real Thing.[2]

Understand, however, that an encounter with the manifest presence of God isn't without a certain cost.

What will happen to your social standing at work and in church if your symptoms begin to defy every attempt at disguise? Are you willing to pay the price of His presence?

Even one holy encounter with Him will permanently alter your perspective of life. Your "condition" won't get any better after you catch Him. You will just get more desperate than before. The glory of His face is addictive in the extreme.

Will you continue the chase if it marks you as a member of the restless remnant who are desperate for yet another God encounter?

If your answer is yes, then you should prepare yourself for a life of uncommon courage and accomplishment in the kingdom. God loves to work through people who dare to believe Him and are determined to pursue Him.

Are you willing to face the "heat" like the three Hebrew children who chose the flames of a furnace over the safety they could enjoy by merely bowing their knees before man's idea of what true worship should be?[3]

PRAYER

My symptoms are showing, Lord. You are beginning to dominate my thoughts, and my hunger for Your presence is getting completely out of hand. I can't help myself. All I want is You, Lord. I will pursue You all the days of my life because my passion leaves me no choice. I'm part of that restless remnant, a chronic God Chaser with an unending appetite for Your presence.

THE SECOND DAY

Just One Look Changes Your Vision Forever

After he caught sight of God taking His seat, Isaiah didn't see things the same way. He didn't say things the same way, and he didn't prophesy the same way.
THE GOD CATCHERS, P. 16

SCRIPTURE READING:

Isaiah 6:1–5, in which a seer observes the King of kings and never views earthly thrones the same way again.

The best king in Isaiah's earthly life succumbed to the seduction of strength and ultimately died in shame and isolation. The prophet lifted his eyes in the temple one day and saw a greater King fill his vision, and suddenly his broken heart was transformed and filled with a burning glory.

The seduction of strength endangers everything in our lives. It can transform a natural gift for athletics, music, science, or business ventures into a deadly idol that threatens to displace God Himself from the throne of our lives.

How many times have you watched someone you loved and respected fall into the depths of failure after succumbing to the seduction of strength? (How many times have you put more trust in your own strength than in God?)

"None of us have room for two kings in our lives."⁴ The King of glory waited until Isaiah's earthly king died before He allowed the prophet to catch Him in the temple. He was saying, in essence, "Now I'll let you see Me. You

24

thought the glory of the former king was incredible; let Me show you *My* glory."[5]

Has God been waiting for some king to die in your life before revealing His manifest presence to you? If you have any doubt about who or what you worship, examine your life. Where do you invest most of your time, energy, money, and appetite?

The good news is that Isaiah made it through the hard times after King Uzziah's death to become one of the greatest Old Testament prophets. As I wrote in *The God Catchers*, "What happened? Isaiah spent thirty seconds in the presence of the King, high and lifted up, and it utterly redirected, reformed, and transformed his life and ministry."[6]

Are there times when you wish your life would be "utterly redirected, reformed, and transformed"? What will it take, and how much are you willing to invest in it?

God will have you only one way—His way. In my first book, *The God Chasers,* I said,

When Moses told God, "Show me Your glory," the Lord said, "You can't, Moses. Only dead men can see My face." Fortunately, Moses didn't stop there. Unfortunately, the Church did.

. . . The God of Moses is willing to reveal Himself to you today, but it is not going to be a "cheap" blessing. You're going to have to lay down and die, and the more you die, the closer He can come.[7]

Just how close do you want Him to come?

Prayer

Lord, I'm not sure where You will take me or how much of "me" will be left in the end. All I know is that I have to be with You. I'm desperate for Your presence, and nothing less will do. Here I am, Lord. Remake and renew me so I will be holy in Your sight.

Brokenness and Dependency Lead to Intimacy

Uzziah's chief sin, and the cause of his unclean flesh, was that he mishandled in presumption the glory of God . . . He knew better; he just chose to do things his own way.

THE GOD CATCHERS, P. 19

SCRIPTURE READING:

2 Chronicles 26:16–19 and Psalm 51:17, in which we see the destruction of presumption and the grace God extends to broken and contrite hearts.

King David and King Uzziah began well, but they ended their courses of life in totally different places.

What happened to these two great kings along the way that separated their destinies in God? (See p. 20 of *The God Catchers*.)

Where David offered brokenness and totally dependent love to God and was invited into God's inner chambers of intimacy, Uzziah assumed he was worthy and barged into God's chambers with an offering immersed in the fragrance of pride, arrogance, and presumption.[8]

What picture formed in your mind when you read this description of King Uzziah? Perhaps you thought, *It's easy to see that King*

Uzziah was headed for disaster. That kind of behavior would never do in God's presence.

If we could ask King Uzziah to describe his behavior, he might put things differently: "As the king, and as the true spiritual leader who led Israel back from spiritual apathy to spiritual revival, I felt it was my sworn duty to bravely enter God's chambers bearing gifts while carrying myself with the self-respect and dignity appropriate for my office."

We like to distance ourselves from any Bible personality who received God's punishment, and it is an art we practice and perfect from our earliest years. "I would never do something as stupid as that . . . I commit little sins once in a while, but nothing like the sin of Uzziah!"

Are you willing to admit that you have done your fair share of "distancing" and justifying in your life? Where or what did it get you?

The truth can become unbearably familiar at times, and the truth is that nearly every one of us has acted like King Uzziah at one time or another. In fact, anytime we approach the Lord outside brokenness or totally dependent love, by default we are party to the Uzziah Syndrome.

Honestly examine your most recent church service, and carefully consider your level of worship and inward conduct during that time. Would you characterize them as broken or whole? As dependent and loving, or as independent and presumptuous toward God?

The problem is that God has no interest in or liking for our independence, and He is rarely if ever attracted to whole, self-sufficient hearts. He is more interested in seeking and finding broken and contrite hearts than in collecting those that show no need for Him.

What are you offering Him right now?

PRAYER

Lord, I would rather be broken and in Your presence than whole and apart from You. I desperately need You in every part of my life. Please forgive me for all of the ways I've rejected You by choosing to cling to my own strengths and abilities.

Exchange Human Arrogance for Holy Heartburn

The only cure for the Uzziah Syndrome is an Isaiah experience with God that you will never get over. Most of us never make it to that point because we get angry when we are confronted with the truth. We get angry instead of yielding to sorrowful repentance, and we insist on swinging our sacred religious censers filled with unauthorized and unacceptable offerings. What we need are burning lips and a hot heart. One coal from His altar will cure our arrogance.

THE GOD CATCHERS, P. 21

SCRIPTURE READING:

Isaiah 6:6–8, where the prophet's unclean lips are purged with a coal from the altar of God's presence.

Most of us would never describe ourselves as arrogant because we have a preconceived idea about what arrogance looks like. The truth is that arrogance doesn't always swagger or speak in overbearing tones. Sometimes it does its work subtly, with sly intent and silent insubordination.

Arrogance often dresses up in priestly robes or our Sunday best, so it can secretly infect our worship like a killer virus. I asked in *The God Catchers:* "Has God turned away from us because of our empty religious forms? Has our presumption polluted our offerings and disqualified us from residence in His presence?" (p. 21).

Can you detect the presence of arrogance in the ways you have worshiped God? How did it affect your time with God?

"The arrogance of adolescence" describes a peculiar disinterest in and disdain of virtually everything that doesn't generate from self. When we grow older in our faith, it seems that we often lose the joy of innocence that marked our early days in Christ. As we "grow up," we tend to grow cynical and critical at the same time.

We adopt a "been there, done that" attitude about the things of God, almost as if we are daring God to amuse or impress us with something newer or more exciting than usual. This attitude often has an all-too-familiar sound: "Oh, it's just You. Oh, it's just church; they're just singing another song. It's just another sermon" (*The God Catchers,* p. 24).

How many ways has the affliction of adolescent arrogance crept up on you in church services? Did you ever sense the warning voice of the Holy Spirit signaling that you had crossed the line?

Many people confuse my message exhorting people to hotly pursue God's presence with the idea that "old is bad" and that God could not and would not speak to us using the things of the past, such as hymns, traditional sermons, church rituals, and so on. They miss the point. God can and does speak through these things when we pursue Him instead of limiting Him to certain things, procedures, or personal preferences.

Has God's presence ever touched you through songs, messages, or methods that you typically avoid or that were totally unfamiliar to you? Do you think He did it on purpose?

Behind every song could be the fresh discovery of His presence. When passionate pleas replace dry discourses, "church" can become the celebration of His presence it was always meant to be. He was always there waiting, but the conditions were not correct. (*The God Catchers,* pp. 24–25)

What does God want you to do to help make it happen?

PRAYER

Lord, forgive me for every arrogant dismissal of people or things in our worship gatherings. I forgot that it is all about You, not about me. By Your grace, I will search for You in every word spoken and every song sung. I will search for You as diligently in the mundane as in the magnificent. All I really want is You. Please deliver me from my adolescent arrogance.

Offer Him Your Broken Heart and See the Heavens Open

When brokenness appears in our lives, openness appears in the heavens.
THE GOD CATCHERS, P. 25

SCRIPTURE READING:
Psalm 34:18–19, in which we see that God is near the brokenhearted.

Human desperation and brokenness are the mortar and stone of heavenly dependence, and they are the integral components of greatness in God. He can use virtually everything that drives us from the limits of our strength, endurance, abilities, and resources to draw us closer to His heart and deeper into His purposes.

If human desperation and brokenness are so important to the purposes of God, how can we remain in a continual state of desperation and brokenness before Him?

One way to remain in a state of heavenly dependency is to change your attitude about hardship and impossibility. By definition, any assignment from God is supernatural. If it is really from God, then you will be unable to accomplish it apart from divine provision and intervention. A scholar cited in the Amplified Bible defines *faith* as "that leaning of the entire human personality on God in absolute trust and confidence."[9] There is no better time or place to lean on Him with all of your being.

32

Do you prefer to pick the easy things you can do for God using your own gifts and abilities, or will you accept assignments from Him that push you far beyond your resources, strength, abilities, and faith level?

It may have been the pain of a funeral that helped Isaiah put all of his dependence on God, but we know he was a changed man after he saw the Lord high and lifted up in the temple. Do you remember this passage in *The God Catchers*?

God will take advantage of your desperate feelings to create a dependency on Him. Thirty seconds in the manifest presence of God can change everything. It can change a nation, it can change your destiny, and it can rearrange your future. You'll never be the same. (p. 25)

What causes you to lift your dependence from your shoulders or the shoulders of another person and place it on the broad shoulders of God? Are you really prepared for a God encounter that will change everything?

PRAYER

Lord, I'm desperate for You. My broken heart and broken dreams, with all of the broken relationships of the past, and the countless broken promises made to me (and that I've made to others and to You)—I offer all of my brokenness to You. Open the heavens and answer my passionate call for Your presence, Lord.

Pursuing the God Who Is Close

In His infiniteness, He could hide where you could never find Him, but He hides in the folds of time so that while you're singing a little song, praying a prayer, you discover Him. He didn't hide far away; He hid close.

THE GOD CATCHERS, P. 27

SCRIPTURE READING:

Acts 17:26–28, where the apostle Paul tells the Grecian philosophers that God "is not far from each one of us."

Most people don't think of hiding from a father's point of view, at least, not until little children invade their lives in some way. Hiding means avoidance to most of us until the child-rearing years. According to "mature" thinking, someone hides only to avoid prosecution for wrongs done or to avoid the potentially dangerous or unpleasant actions of pursuers and predators (such as muggers), or of persistent pests (such as unpleasant or nosy neighbors). The very idea of hiding to be found is foreign to most of us until we are required to entertain, care for, or raise children.

If someone had told you several years ago, "God hides from us," would your reaction have been the same then as it would be today? If so, is it that you once believed God hides from us to avoid us, or that He doesn't hide at all?

People seeking to avoid someone really try to hide as far away as possible. Parents, on the other hand, generally understand the need to hide so they can be found. When our heavenly Father hides from us, He understands the necessity of hiding close. After all, His goal is to be found, not lost.

When God feels far away from you, the reality is that He is hiding very close to you. Your passionate need for Him and the isolation you feel during the time of separation make you all the more attractive to Him.

How does this change the way you approach the Lord? If God is close to you in your times of need, how do you get Him to reveal His manifest presence?

Remember that He hides so that He can be found. "You can find Him in worship. Your passion is how you discover Him. Passion—not perfection—pulls God from His dimension into yours" (*The God Catchers*, p. 27).

Many of us seem to mimic the stereotypical elementary school child delivering a prepared speech before the class when we call on God. We focus on the position of our feet. Are they perfectly aligned? Are our toes pointing outward? How about our posture? Are the shoulders back, and the back straight? Is everything just right? Are we using formal English language forms with proper enunciation techniques? Details, details, details—it almost seems that form and not content matters the most to us.

If you reposition that stereotypical child to the privacy of his own home and give him a need that only his daddy can fulfill, all of his concerns about posture, form, language, and propriety are forgotten in a heartbeat. "It's time to run to Daddy; I'm hurting, and he doesn't give demerits for improper syntax or flawed delivery. All he cares about is me!" Where Daddy is concerned, it is content and relationship over form and outward appearance!

How do you approach "Abba, Father" in times of great need?[10]

Each day as you pursue His presence, remember these points from *The God Catchers:*

There really is no formula. We have allowed the structure of man to impede the passion of a child. That's why the Master Teacher said, "Assuredly, I say to you, unless you are converted and become as little children, you will by no means enter the kingdom of heaven." (p. 28)

PRAYER

Abba, Father, I need You. You are the only One who can supply what I so desperately need. I thank You for Your countless gifts and blessings, but what I want the most is You. I know You are close to me, but I want to see Your face.

Pursue Him, Your Single Magnificent Obsession!

It is time to allow the king of all other pursuits to die. Let the pursuit of His presence become your single magnificent obsession.

THE GOD CATCHERS, P. 30

SCRIPTURE READING:

Matthew 22:36–37, where Jesus reminds us to love God with all within us.

Most obsessions (as with all but one addiction) are considered abnormal and potentially dangerous at times. Thousands of people go through life with what psychiatrists and psychologists call an *obsessive-compulsive disorder* (OCD). The actions of individuals with OCD often seem to exemplify the dictionary definition of *obsession:* "a persistent disturbing preoccupation with an often unreasonable idea or feeling; compelling motivation."[11]

Hearing this may shock you, but the Bible commands us to embrace one specific obsession. Jesus said to him, "You shall love the LORD your God with *all* your heart, with *all* your soul, and with *all* your mind."[12]

Are you obsessed with God or just mildly enamored of Him? Rate your obsession with God on a "temperature" scale of 1 to 5, with 5 being the hottest. Where do you stand? Are you hot, cold, or worst of all, lukewarm?

What an irony! The best way I've found to describe our proper relationship to God is to use a word reserved for abnormal preoccupation and compelling motivations!

Somehow the terms *apathy, conservative,* and *laid-back* just don't seem to apply to the proper pursuit of God. Unfortunately they apply all too well to the way we actually deal with God personally and corporately in the church.

God is calling for change in the church. We must return to our first love by making the pursuit of His presence our "single magnificent obsession." I can tell you right now that the task is too difficult for you to handle on your own. The good news is that the impossible is genuinely possible "for it is God who works in you both to will and to do for His good pleasure."[13]

Are you really prepared to see your life transformed into a lifestyle of holy addiction, godly obsession, and righteous possession in the pursuit of His presence? What will it cost you? What will you gain?

It will be worth it if "like Moses, you've seen a lot of things, but you really want one thing more than any other."[14]

PRAYER

Show us Your glory, Lord. We seek Your face in our immaturity. We don't really know how to do it, but we know You are here. We are desperately hunting for You.[15]

I Don't Know Whether to Laugh or Cry

Caught in the Middle of What Is and What Can Be

Uncertain and unable to move one step more, you are caught in the middle of what is and what can be. At the end of yourself with nothing but the promise of faith and hope in your heart, you are in a good place. You may not know whether to laugh or cry, but it doesn't matter because it is in His hands now.

Embrace Hunger and Avoid Infatuation with Satisfaction

Sometimes I think that satisfaction may be the greatest enemy of the purposes of God in the church and in the world.

THE GOD CATCHERS, P. 32

SCRIPTURE READING:

Revelation 3:15–17, in which the Lord warns the church about the dangers of the lukewarm life and confident satisfaction with earthly success.

The Christian life gets difficult when we emphasize the importance of our physical senses and appetites more than our pursuit of God. The problem is that our senses seem to have a louder voice than God's still small voice. I'm convinced that He planned it that way.

The ability of human beings to feel physical pain, hunger, sensual stimulation, and fatigue comes naturally from the earliest moments in the womb. Our ability to sense His presence, hear His voice, and discern between good and evil comes more slowly and at a certain price. We must choose to pursue God and His kingdom, unlike our innate and automatic ability to sense things in the natural realm.

Have you noticed how you unconsciously sense hunger, thirst, danger, and desire in the natural realm, but must consciously pursue them in the spiritual realm?

The pursuit of God yields countless blessings in both the spiritual and the natural realms when He turns to pursue us. Satisfaction and abundant provision often accompany or follow hungry pursuit. There is nothing wrong with this unless we stop our pursuit to celebrate over our blessings while leaving behind all thoughts of the Blesser!

Far too many God Chasers stop the chase to celebrate their best pace in the last race. We forget to resume the pursuit when we stop to build monuments to a momentary visitation of God's presence. (*The God Catchers,* p. 32)

Can you recall any time that you suspended the chase for God to build a monument to something He did in your life? What happened to the anointing and joy of His presence during that time?

The problem isn't the satisfaction supplied by God's blessings; it is our tendency to prefer His blessings over the pursuit of the Blesser. We find it much easier to rest in His blessings and reminisce about past races than to put on our God Chaser shoes and pursue Him and His purposes with all of our might.

If anyone could have stopped the race to be satisfied with his accomplishments, it would have been Paul. Yet he felt compelled by love to invest his life for Christ time and again in places he had never been, among people he'd never met. We find it nearly impossible to invest one hour in our own community among people we've known all our lives!

Think about Paul's ministry and all of the insights God provided through his ministry and his epistles to the churches. List some of the consequences if Paul had halted his chase to celebrate his successes. Now consider the consequences if you do the same things.

Jesus described the chilling satisfaction syndrome afflicting the church in the book of Revelation: "You say, 'I am rich, have become wealthy, and have need of nothing'—and do not know that you are wretched, miserable, poor, blind, and naked."[1]

God's reaction to this brand of Christianity is so extreme and final that I'm sure many people would like to remove it from their Bibles: "So then, because you are lukewarm, and neither cold nor hot, I will vomit you out of My mouth."[2]

How do you plan to avoid the pitfalls of infatuation with satisfaction?

"It is hunger that *keeps* us in the pursuit" (*The God Catchers*, p. 32).

PRAYER

Lord, may I find satisfaction only in the light of Your presence. I don't want to find solace only in my memories of past visitations and encounters with You. I want to be with You now, and again tomorrow, and forevermore.

Welcome to the House of the Very Grateful and the Very Desperate

Hunger is among the most attractive things we have to offer to our Creator.

[ADAPTED FROM] *THE GOD CATCHERS*, P. 33

SCRIPTURE READING:

Ezra 3:11–13, where the prophet Ezra describes a strange mix of joy and sorrow revealed at the temple groundbreaking.

God's household can take on strange appearances at times. The newest generation of God Chasers rejoices at His slightest appearing while the most senior saints filter and measure every manifestation against the watermarks of previous visitations. Both are right and both are wrong, and wisdom is found wherever the two meet, share, and move forward together.

Have you noticed the different ways people around you react when the presence of God manifests among you? Have you caught yourself reacting with skepticism when you knew you should have been rejoicing?

Younger Chasers are quick to rejoice at the slightest manifestation of God's glory, and that is good. Yet they are often surprised and overwhelmed after the temporary glory fades to be replaced by the heat of trials and opposition. They are also prone to stop at their last visitation to build monuments unless instructed by wise God Catchers that there is more.

Are you personally acquainted with the tendency to fade under the heat of adversity, or to stop the pursuit to build a cabinet to hold yesterday's God Chaser trophy?

Elder saints are prone to hold their applause until they can gauge the depth and validity of the appearance of Divinity. This has an element of wisdom, but it can easily be transformed into cynical doubt and unbelief that hinder and endanger the faith of younger believers. Very few sins are more serious than this! According to all three synoptic Gospels, Jesus reserved talk of "millstones around the neck" and drowning at sea for those foolish individuals who lay stumbling blocks for God's kids.[3]

Are you surprised by God's reaction to stumbling-block Christians? Have you ever been tripped up by the cynicism of others? (Have you ever tripped others through your words or actions?)

It is said that the greatest obstacle to the latest move of God is the generation that experienced the previous move of the Spirit, and history confirms it. God obviously has a better plan. He intends for the older saints to guide, instruct, encourage, and support younger saints in their passionate pursuit of God.[4] Anything less is sin.[5]

Much of our problem has been the church's satisfaction with less than God's best. Even our language reflects our attraction to mediocrity and middle-of-the-road commitment:

We tend to satisfy our hunger pains through the performance of minor religious duties such as once-a-week church attendance or an occasional prayer on the run. Hunger has ceased to be part of our religious vocabulary because it is considered "undignified" by today's spiritual elite. (*The God Catchers*, p. 33)

Are you prepared to be "undignified" in the eyes of the spiritual elite? Are you willing to survive on starvation rations of one scant meal per week, or will you pay the cost to passionately pursue Him and enjoy the bounty of His presence more and more?

PRAYER

Lord, I will be undignified if it means I can stand by Your side or sit at Your feet in the joy of Your presence. My food is not found in the approval and applause of men or women; my meat is to do Your will, and my drink is to pursue Your presence with all of my strength.

Restoring the Proper Posture of the Church

Ezra said the noise of the weepers and the noise of the rejoicers could not be distinguished from each other. I propose that this is the proper posture for the church. We are grateful for what He has done, but we are also desperate for what He can do. *This odd mix of joy with sorrow, of satisfaction with hunger, is common wherever God shows up.*

THE GOD CATCHERS, P. 35

SCRIPTURE READING:

2 Chronicles 7:14–16, in which God promises to heal the land of those who will humble themselves, pray, and seek His face.

God seems to be seeking people who know how to be grateful and desperate at the same time. These God Chasers become God Catchers when they discover the secrets of genuine repentance married to true worship. The inevitable fruit of this marriage is the "joy inexpressible and full of glory."[6]

It is easier to figure out the proverbial "chicken or the egg" question than to determine which comes first: godly sorrow or divine joy? godly satisfaction or holy hunger? They could be called the Siamese twins of the Spirit, inseparable yet clearly distinct.

Does this sound strange to you, or have you experienced the combination of godly sorrow and divine joy; and godly satisfaction and holy hunger? Which came first? Is it always that way?

Nearly all can agree that King David was a genuine God Chaser. His writings in the Psalms indicate that he knew the heights of holy communion with

God, yet he also knew the depths of godly sorrow leading to repentance. Both components helped deliver him into God's presence, and both were the products of His appearing.

At times, God's manifested presence reduces an assembly of worshipers to tears and heart-wrenching repentance. The very next moment, He may lift them to new heights of heavenly joy—even while their hot tears still run down their cheeks. The key point to remember is that it is all God's doing in times of true visitation and holy habitation. Man's manipulation is not welcome when Father is in the house (nor should it be welcome at any other time).

Has the presence of God ever moved you to sorrowful repentance? Has His presence ignited supernatural joy in your life? What did the two encounters share in common?

In whatever season you find yourself, always seek His face for more. If you can do nothing but repent before Him on bended knee or with your tear-stained face pressed to the floor, then do it with all of your might. But look for the day when "times of refreshing may come from the presence of the Lord."[7]

If His presence seems to seize your feet and send them dancing for joy, then dance before Him with all of your might as David did. At the same time, look forward to the season of repentance and soul-searching, for God loves to reward those who seek true righteousness and holiness in His honor.[8]

If He is the Potter and we are the clay, then we should expect to alternate between seasons of pressure as He molds us into a shape of His choosing, and seasons of refreshing when He showers us with His refreshing presence to restore elasticity to our frame.[9] It is the only way we can accommodate the stretching of our human hearts by divine hands.

Have you ever wanted to step off the Potter's wheel, even though you knew it was where you were supposed to be? Was staying put worth it once the season of molding was over?

Perhaps now we better understand why "it is entirely possible and even desirable for us to be grateful and desperate at the same time" (adapted from *The God Catchers*, pp. 34–35).

PRAYER

Lord, I thank You for what You've done, but I am desperate for what I know You can do! I'm taking my position squarely between the weeping post of repentance and intercession, and the dancing floor of rejoicing. Move me from one to the other as it pleases You. Above all, let me see Your glory!

Go Ahead: Laugh and Cry (You're in a Good Place)

Once you reach the point where it is all you can do to maintain your composure, my question is, Why try?

THE GOD CATCHERS, P. 36

SCRIPTURE READING:

Proverbs 27:6, in which we learn that even the blows of a friend are better than the kisses of an enemy. (That should give us a hint about how to view correction and instruction from the One we pursue.)

There is a certain security for God Chasers who come to the end of themselves. Understanding this is important because becoming a God Chaser (or even a God Catcher from time to time) offers no guarantee that trouble or difficulty won't come your way. In fact, God's Word guarantees it will arrive at your address. Paul said, "All who desire to live godly in Christ Jesus will suffer persecution."[10]

Have you read this passage before? Even if you have, does the reality of Paul's words still possess the "voltage" to shock you into a new level of thoughtfulness and reevaluation? (Do you think God planned it that way?)

True God Chasers have no regard for pie-in-the-sky theologies or false concepts of rose garden discipleship. If life is that easy all of the time, then there may be more of you than of Him at the center of it all. He is the God who

49

loves, sacrifices, and gives much; those who follow Him must be prepared to do the same.

God Chasers don't chase comfort, although they often receive it in abundance. They don't even chase joy, although it is theirs almost without limit. They don't chase the gifts, provisions, and prosperity of God, although they are all delightful, necessary, and much appreciated. God Chasers ask for them when necessary and where required in the Scriptures, but their chief desire is set on Him and His manifested glory. (They know that everything else comes with Him anyway.)

Compare Matthew 6:33 and 1 Corinthians 14:12. In the first, Jesus *commanded* us to seek first the kingdom of God and His righteousness while trusting that everything else will come besides. In the second, Paul began by saying, "Since you are zealous for spiritual gifts . . ." In other words, we are *permitted* to seek the gifts that most edify the body; although under normal circumstances, it seems that gifts are freely given to all at the discretion of the Spirit for the benefit of all (see 1 Cor. 12:7).

If these passages offended you, do you know why? Did they catch your attention because some of these characteristics apply to your life? What do you sense the Holy Spirit is saying about it?

It is inevitable that at many points in the chase, a God Chaser must come to the end of himself. Most of the time it comes at the point where human strength and ability end and divine provision begins. At other times the end comes when obstacles or storms stirred up by the adversary overwhelm a God Chaser and make him despair for life and hope—but for the grace of God. To be honest, the end sometimes comes because of our own sin, delay, disobedience, fear, or unresolved problems we refuse to let God solve.

Have you ever reached the end of yourself only to ask, Is it just me? Am I destined for failure, or is there more? Sometimes it's good to ask those questions, but where did you go from there?

Regardless of how you reach the end of yourself, God is able to transform it into a new beginning and gateway to joy. I read somewhere that "all things work together for good to those who love God, to those who are the called according to His purpose."[11] I'm convinced that "when you don't know whether to laugh or cry, you may be in a good place" (*The God Catchers,* p. 36).

> We should be reassured and encouraged when God brings us to the point where we don't know whether to laugh or cry. If nothing else, it means that God is at work in you "both to will and to do for His good pleasure." A holy hunger is being fired up inside you that will take you to the edge of dissatisfaction and joy at the same time. (*The God Catchers,* pp. 35–36)

Are you at the end of yourself right now? Have you hit bottom so hard that you don't know whether to laugh or cry? (Or maybe someone you know is at the end of himself.) God is at work, and He has more than failure in store.

Prayer

Lord, it has come to this: I don't have anything left to give. I'm tired, discouraged, and over my head in troubled waters. If You don't show up, no one else should even bother. I'm hungry for You—at any cost. Nothing less than You will do this time. I don't need just a miracle; I'm after the Miracle Worker Himself! I'm on the edge of ragged dissatisfaction and unspeakable joy, and I'm determined to cross over the line.

Pursuing an Incurable God Addiction

John's "God addiction" isn't something to be scorned; it is something to be sought after and duplicated in our own lives.

THE GOD CATCHERS, P. 39

SCRIPTURE READING:

John 13:24–25; 21:20–22, where John is described as "the disciple whom Jesus loved" and the one Peter asked to question Jesus about the betrayer.

The stereotypes begin early: "He's a mama's boy," or "She's just a daddy's girl." Many times the children who receive these labels are only children or the youngest child in the family, and may be considered the weakest in the family.

Stereotypes affect the more mature as well. Christians have been called weak and disabled by those who scornfully referred to God as their "crutch." In this case, our critics are absolutely, delightfully, incredibly correct!

All we like sheep have gone astray;
We have turned, every one, to his own way;
And the Lord has laid on Him the iniquity of us all.[12]

He said to me, "My grace is sufficient for you, for My strength is made perfect in weakness." Therefore most gladly I will rather boast in my infirmities, that the power of Christ may rest upon me.[13]

Can you relate to some of these childhood and adult stereotypes? Are you ready to accept what many in the world and in the church think is a negative stereotype just for the sake of the chase? Is it really that important to you to pursue His presence?

In God's kingdom, a unique place of honor and authority is reserved for the weakest, the least, the humble and broken in heart, those who hunger and thirst, the rejected, the last, and the lowly. We seem to do our best to ignore them from the pulpit and the pew, but something about these conditions of human weakness attracts God's manifested presence and divine strength.[14]

As I noted in *The God Catchers,*

It sure seems to me that Jesus was telling us to remain in a perpetual state of asking, seeking, and knocking. What I don't see in the New Testament is any command requiring us (or even permitting us) to be complacent, apathetic, or lethargic. (p. 37)

Is your life marked by perpetual asking, seeking, and knocking for more of God? What would you call it if your life reveals anything less?

We should take our cue from John the disciple, who evidently didn't miss a single night's sleep over the disapproval of his fellow disciples. He wasn't a troublemaker or a loner, but he clearly cared more about the opinion of Jesus than the opinions and approval of everyone else combined. What would happen to our lives and churches if we began to do the same? Yes, we should love, honor, and serve our brothers and sisters and reach out to the lost; but God never intended for us to guide our lives or ministries by public opinion or approval ratings.

How do you develop the ability to turn away from human disapproval and criticism and pursue God's approval?

John the Beloved had one strategy in his adult life and ministry: where God was concerned, he would always go straight for the heart. That is a great definition of a God Chaser and of a successful God Catcher.

We can safely assume that John didn't care if the other disciples talked about him, belittled him, or expressed their jealousy over his shameless search for more of the Lord's love. All he knew was that if the Master was within touching distance, then he would go straight for the heart. (*The God Catchers,* p. 39)

PRAYER

Lord, I've gone too far to turn back now. I'm desperate for Your presence, and I'm willing to spend my life pursuing You just for the joy of one more moment in Your manifested glory and grace.

Rediscover the Power of God-ward Passion

When you pray with persistence, worship with abandon, or fast in hunger and desperation, you create heavenly urgency and passion that are virtually irresistible to your Maker and heavenly Father.

THE GOD CATCHERS, P. 40

SCRIPTURE READING:

Revelation 3:17–19, where Jesus commands us to be zealous and repent as a condition for sharing a meal with Him (v. 20).

Many people in the church may be tempted to scoff at the idea of creating heavenly urgency and passion that are virtually irresistible to God. However, people who still feel the painful ecstasy of love for a spouse or fiancé understand what I'm talking about. In the middle of an average and otherwise forgettable day, a longing may seize them to see and hold the beloved. It makes no sense, but who said logic has anything to do with it? This is the domain of love and passion. Those in the grip of love will go to incredible lengths of sacrifice and expense just to spend a few moments with each other.

Where God is concerned, are you in the grip of love or the bondage of boredom? To what length will you go for a few more moments in His presence?

On a higher level, you may find yourself going through the motions of your daily work routine or a typical church service when a deep longing seizes your soul. In one moment, everything changes. Something transforms your prayers from forgettable recitations to passionate appeals to your Beloved.

Worship comes alive with fresh urgency and unbearable longing. Passion begins to color even the most mundane activities in your life. Everything you do, say, and think takes on a new and vibrant focus—an encounter with Deity.

Consider your daily routine and describe your life focus now. Is it everything it should be?

God seems to appear most often where He is wanted. He obviously reaches out to those who don't want Him or who don't even acknowledge that He exists—that is the wonder of the Cross—yet He wants to dwell (the nonchurchy reading might be "hang out") among people who desperately want His presence. That is why Jesus said the Father seeks out worshipers.[15] True God Chasers are like David. They want to hang out in His presence and soak in His glory forever.[16]

Where do you want to hang out the most? Are you more comfortable in front of the TV or in His presence?

If you want to pass beyond the symbolic barrier of the veil of separation and into God's presence in the Holy of Holies, then don't look to logic and intellect to get you there. They "have their proper place, but it is not in the intimacy of the Holy of Holies" (*The God Catchers,* p. 40).

I think we've become too familiar with the pleasure of His provisions and the blessings of His hand. We've forsaken the tears of repentance and passionate desperation known by the revered saints of the past. It is time to rediscover the power of passionate and fervent prayer. (*The God Catchers,* p. 41)

If Jesus reflects the nature of the Godhead as Paul claimed, then we have all the proof we need that we serve a passionate God who knows how to weep, mourn, rejoice, and be zealous and angry for all of the right reasons.[17]

Are you ready to move past religion's empty platitudes and passionless pretense? Embrace the good things in the church but aspire to go higher and deeper into God's presence. Will you dare to bare your desperation and display your passion for His presence?

PRAYER

Lord, teach me how to pray. Forgive me for my prayerlessness and presumption in days gone by. Impart to me the power and passion of fervent prayer so I may seek You with urgency and effectively pray into being Your will on earth as it is in heaven.

It Takes Passion to Attract His Presence

Remember that when passion reenters the church, His presence comes back through the door as well.

THE GOD CATCHERS, P. 43

SCRIPTURE READING:

Psalm 95:6–7, in which the sheep are called to worship and bow down before the Good Shepherd (and enter His rest).

Perhaps it is no accident that on the seventh day we consider what happens when passion reenters the church closely followed by God's presence. It appears that God rests in an atmosphere of pure worship, praise, and adoration. The Bible says He is enthroned in or inhabits the praises of His people.[18]

What kind of throne have you constructed for Him? Does your local church construct a throne for Him each time it gathers in His name, or does it concentrate on another form, structure, or plan?

When David offered to build God a physical house like a temple, the Lord made it clear He did not dwell in temples made by men. Instead He promised to build David's house![19] David's son, Solomon, finally built a grand temple in Jerusalem, but even Solomon knew God wouldn't live there. He simply asked that God answer the prayers offered in that place.[20]

Solomon's lavish temple was later destroyed, but centuries later God said,

On that day I will raise up
The tabernacle of David, which has fallen down,

And repair its damages;
I will raise up its ruins,
And rebuild it as in the days of old.[21]

With all of the biblical evidence at hand, we should know by now that

none of us can build a church building that is pretty enough to attract God. No congregation can accumulate enough stained glass, construct a steeple tall enough, present music that is beautiful enough, or provide enough good preaching to pull Him from His throne in heaven. (*The God Catchers*, p. 42)

If God isn't impressed or moved by these things, are they evil? Whom do they bless if they don't specifically bless Him? Is this wrong as long as we first bless Him?

God is looking for what He found in David's unimpressive tent on a hill: passionate praise and worship from fervent hearts. As I noted in my book *God's Favorite House:* "David's tabernacle was His 'favorite house' because of its unveiled worship of intimacy. It is this atmosphere of intimacy that creates a place of divine habitation—a 'throne zone' on earth as in Heaven—God's favorite house."[22]

Passion and first-person intimacy seemed to characterize David's worship and service before God. Whatever he did for Him, he did it with all of his might.[23] If we do the same, we may learn the secret of leaving our worship gatherings feeling hungrier for His presence than when we came. As I stated in *The God Catchers,* "His chief interest is in your desperation, hunger, and passion for His presence. *He is not after performance; He wants passion*" (p. 43).

PRAYER

Lord, let us leave Your presence more hungry than when we came in. May we always be grateful but desperate; thankful but still hungry. May our first and last prayer to You eternally be, "I'm hungry for You!"[24]

Shall We Gather at the River or Just Jump In?

The Perils of Valuing Program Above Presence

Millions of Christians sense an inner invitation to something closer to the heart of God. The standard forms and patterns of man's worship are neither the source of the call nor the solution to the longing it birthed.

Nevertheless, when the pursuit of His presence takes them to the outer boundaries of the accepted and usual church programs, many hesitate on the bank, fearing the unknown element of faith and the cost of obedience.

Lord, deliver us from the fear of man and the bondage of unbiblical traditions.

THE FIRST DAY

Shall We Waver at the River?

The Israelites in the wilderness chose to embrace all the negative reports and the "safe" counsel of men instead of the "riskier" counsel of God. As a result, an entire generation died homeless. They never stepped into the water of transition from the deliverance of bondage to the possession of God's promise. It's time for this generation to dive into the river.

THE GOD CATCHERS, P. 46, EMPHASIS MINE

SCRIPTURE READING:

Numbers 13:17–14:38 and Hebrews 3:14–4:1, where we discover the danger of wavering in unbelief when God commands us to jump into His purpose by faith.

People who follow the living God move forward constantly. As a follower and a chaser, you know that if you expect to follow Him, then rivers are not purely recreation stations where you can dip your toes in the water while remaining securely on the apparent safety of the bank. As God Chasers, we all must understand that "rivers are to cross and transition through" (*The God Catchers*, p. 46).

When you are going nowhere and have nothing to accomplish, then wavering, hesitating, and stalling become a way of life. If you dare to deny your fears and selfish motives and instead pick up your cross and chase the Savior, then crossings, transitions, changes, and challenges are your constant companions.[1] Stopping midstream and looking back are not options for you.[2] If you choose to live this kind of life, then it becomes mandatory that you live by faith.[3]

Have you done your share of wavering at the river? Are you ready to cross the waters of uncertainty and possess God's purpose for

your life, no matter what the cost? Describe what some of the cost may be.

There is nothing wrong with stained glass or well-trained choirs, and preaching is obviously a thoroughly biblical foundation of the Christian life. However, I don't mean to burst a cherished bubble, but God isn't impressed with any of these things. *They are for us,* not Him. (*The God Catchers,* p. 47)

According to Paul, Jesus gave the leadership gifts of apostle, prophet, evangelist, pastor, and teacher to the church for one major reason: to equip the saints for the work of the ministry.[4] This is where we find the proper place and function of preaching, teaching, exhortation, instruction, and discipleship.

Our problem is that we've grown so fond of our earthly teachers, classrooms, and curriculum that we refuse to graduate from God's prep school and enter the spiritual workplace (the harvest). In other words, we are wavering on the riverbank of temporary comfort and refuse to cross by faith into the land of purpose and promise.

It is not my place to predict what will happen, but we do know that when the Israelites pulled the same stunt, they exchanged their promise from God for a lifetime of purposeless wandering. That was what I was referring to when I said,

He comes to our meetings only in response to our worship and our hunger. Remember that earthly brokenness creates heavenly openness. For that reason, I am compelled by the Spirit of God to say what may be one of the oddest statements you will ever see in a Christian book:

Don't let church obscure your view of God. (*The God Catchers,* p. 47)

Do you think a biblical church—one framed and operated on the true New Testament model—would obscure your view of God? Does the church of this generation obscure and block the passionate pursuit of God, or does it fan the flames of God-ward passion and urge forward everyone who would pursue Him?

Our chief function within the church is to love and worship God, and our secondary internal function is to build up, encourage, and love one another.[5]

Our chief function outside the church is to be a witness to the city, to the whole nation and neighboring countries, and to the end of the world and make disciples of all nations.[6]

In your study of God's Word, have you ever found the task of "Pleasing Self" noted on God's list? So who put it there? Since the apostle Paul told us to examine and test ourselves,[7] ask yourself, If I remove that illegal entry from my God Chasing list, how am I doing as a disciple of Christ? How is my local church doing?[8]

Prayer

Dear Lord, by Your grace I will deny myself daily, take up my cross, and chase after You. Grant me the grace to be graceful to those who refuse to chase with me, or who may even try to hinder my pursuit of Your presence. Have mercy on the church, and continue Your purifying work in the church, Lord. We desperately need You.

God Doesn't Do Out of the Box Revival

God has to break through our programs before He can break out and manifest His presence among us. He has to demolish our artificial intelligence (our dim and sometimes haughty imitation of His omniscience) and artificial spirituality (our programs) to bring in the real thing and take a city or nation.

Unfortunately it is a rare church that can handle the divine call to self-demolition and reignition by the fire of God.

THE GOD CATCHERS, P. 48

SCRIPTURE READING:

John 2:13–17, in which Jesus turns the tables on the religious marketplace and reveals His politically incorrect passion for the Father's house.

No one seems to know whether our fixation with repetitive formulas and fixed equations stems from our earliest experiences in elementary schoolrooms or from our innate search for unchanging security in our ever-changing world. (It makes me wonder why people don't set their sights on the unchanging God of eternity instead of the lowly world of human repetition.)

In what areas can you see this compulsion for sameness operating in your life? Is it necessarily wrong? Does it belong in your times of praise and worship to God?

Professional athletes do it when they carefully tuck a lucky rabbit's foot in a pocket or wear a lucky T-shirt from the 1996 championship season under a uniform for every game. Why? They want to experience the same success they experienced in 1996.

Marketing researchers do it every time they design an advertisement or product package using tried and proven colors, shapes, and appeals that worked the year before.

Churches and worshipers do it when they insist on reproducing the exact song, the same order of service, or the prime preaching mode that worked last year or in another city where revival broke out. We instinctively repackage the success of yesterday to produce a program for today in the hope that somehow it will bring revival.

Have you ever seen this "repackage the anointing" mode at work in your life or anywhere else in the Christian world? What were the results? Did God reveal His manifest glory because of these things or in spite of them?

It seems to me that in light of our habitual repackaging and programming tactics, God will go out of His way *not* to endorse them by showing up. Why? His track record throughout history reveals His ancient hatred for anything that separates Him from His children. That includes anything and everything that encourages us to take Him for granted or act presumptuously toward things holy (and I can't think of a better definition for this bad habit of dressing up memories of yesterday's visitations as today's manifestations).

He wants to preserve the joy and freshness of our encounters together, and equations and formulas do exactly the opposite.

. . . God wants to "break outside of the box." That means that our hunger has to get bigger than the religious box we've built over multiplied centuries of man-centered religious practice. We must have an uncontainable hunger to entertain our uncontainable God. That automatically disqualifies the religious program. (*The God Catchers*, pp. 49–50)

Are you tired of trying to satisfy your spiritual hunger on the meager feast provided by yesterday's revelations and visitations? Is your hunger great enough to propel you past the obstacles of tradition, rigid programs, and lowered expectations? Will you let Him overturn your table of religious trinkets in return for the Real Thing?

PRAYER

We need the Real Thing, Lord. We need nothing more or less than You. Deliver us from ourselves and from our endless imitations of true visitation by Your presence, Lord. Complete the good work You began in us. Break out of our boxes of presumption, overturn our religious tables, and reveal Your glory to our hungry hearts. We are desperate for You.

You Can Have It Only One Way: Man's Glory or God's Glory

We have the unfortunate habit of offering worship to the instrument instead of to the divine Player of the earthly instrument. And I read somewhere that "no flesh should glory in His presence."

THE GOD CATCHERS, P. 51

SCRIPTURE READING:

1 Corinthians 1:27–29, in which God shames the wise with the foolish, and the mighty with the weak, so that no flesh will glory in His presence.

The church often makes one fundamental mistake in its attempts to accommodate and welcome the presence of God: it allows flesh to share the glory while expecting God to manifest Himself in its meetings. It will never happen. The Scriptures couldn't be any clearer about God's attitude toward prancing flesh. He will not allow flesh to glory in His presence. Only one kind of glory can occupy the space in our meeting places at any given time: man's glory or God's glory.

Church leaders in particular face a strong temptation to take just a little of the credit whenever God's manifest presence invades a meeting. The moment they do, invariably the Holy Spirit is grieved and His presence leaves.

Have you seen evidence of prancing flesh in meetings you've attended or conducted? How did it affect the atmosphere of the meetings? What glory dominated those meetings: the glory of God or the glory of man?

Think about what God meant when He talked about the wise and foolish through Paul's first epistle to the Corinthians. What it means is that any genuine manifestation of God's presence should probably be attributed to our foolishness and weakness, not to any strengths or abilities we believe we possess.

The truth is that God generally shows up in spite of us, not because of us. The only exception seems to be when we humble ourselves and boldly display our inherent weaknesses, our desperate hunger, and our unapologetic dependency upon Him.

Paul the apostle, for instance, didn't glory in his considerable intellectual and spiritual assets; he made it clear they were no better than garbage in his view.[9] He had eyes only for God, not for himself.

In your opinion, what would be most attractive to God: a church full of hungry, desperate worshipers with no agenda but the cry of dependency upon Divinity, or a church filled with proud, pampered, and picky spiritual smorgasbord samplers seeking another thrill?

Everywhere I go, I hear people setting up "a juvenile howl of the hungry that declares in no uncertain terms, 'No, we don't want you to *talk* about Him anymore. Keep the empty promises and give us the real thing. We want to meet Him! Where do we go and what do we do?'" (*The God Catchers,* p. 50).

Nothing on earth can equal an encounter with the manifest presence of God, so why do we settle for so much less (especially if it is a poor man-made substitute for what only God can supply)? As I noted in *The God Catchers:*

> When Grecian Jews who came to Jerusalem to celebrate the Passover Feast heard that Jesus was nearby, they went to Philip and said, "Sir, we wish to see Jesus."[10] These men knew about the promise of Passover and the theology of theoretical forgiveness, but they wanted to meet Him who was the Passover Lamb. They obviously appreciated Philip's capacity to help them gain access to the Master, but they recognized the difference between a follower of Christ and Christ Himself. *This is the revolution that births revival.*[11]

PRAYER

We want You, Lord Jesus. We've had our fill of empty talk and the fancy prose of men. Father, Sir, we wish to see Jesus. We appreciate all of the men and women You've provided who love and lead us in Your anointing; but we are determined to pursue You and not merely Your messengers. Thank You for theology and theory, but we are after nothing less than the manifestation of Your presence!

Will This Be the Night He Shows Up Again?

If you've ever had encounters with Him, then "man meetings" will drive you crazy because you will be interested only in "God encounters" after that. That is the exact name and address of my God addiction.

THE GOD CATCHERS, P. 52

SCRIPTURE READING:

Luke 24, in which two discouraged disciples experience an encounter with the resurrected Christ that leaves them permanently afflicted with heaven's heartburn and a hunger for more.

The Bible says we are all pilgrims or aliens in this world; we are just passing through to our true eternal destiny.[12] Many people use this concept to justify their disengagement from the world and total inactivity as Christian witnesses to the lost. As far as I can tell, God gave us the light so we could shine brightly enough to illuminate the entire world with His presence. We are to be a glorious city situated on a hill, not a hidden city buried in the valley of compromise or asceticism.[13] We should know by now that God visits and abides with us so we can give away His gifts, blessings, and presence to others in need.

Are you burning brightly or barely glowing with His glory? What do you have in your life that would shine brightly enough to attract people to the God you serve and convince them of His power and love? Theology, sophisticated argumentation, practiced

71

and artificially sustained excitement, or a sense of His presence that accompanies you everywhere you go?

My first book, *The God Chasers,* includes the story of the day my wife went to a store in Houston, Texas, during God's visitation there.[14] She experienced a totally unexpected divine appointment while waiting in a checkout line. The stranger standing behind her with tears streaming down her face tapped on my wife's shoulder and said, "I don't know where you've been, and I don't know what you've got. But my husband is a lawyer and I'm in the middle of a divorce." She continued her story for a moment and finally blurted out, "What I'm really saying is, I need God."

At that point, this woman's desperation and hunger outweighed every concern about public opinion. Nevertheless, she did take time to ask the woman behind her if it was okay that my wife prayed with her right there in the checkout line. The second woman was also crying by then, and she said, "Yes, and pray with me too."

Those women weren't touched by my wife's outward appearance or actions. They were touched by the presence of God that accompanied her right into that store. Divine appointments like that one may not happen every day, but why shouldn't they?

Have you ever experienced a genuine manifestation of the presence of God? What happened to your passion for the unsaved? Did it grow stronger or weaker? What happened to your boldness as a witness for Christ? Did you grow bolder or more timid?

We seem to be more interested in re-creating the secret meetings of the first century in Jerusalem (minus the persecution that made the secrecy necessary). For the most part, we unintentionally leave the lost out of the picture by placing our central focus on blessing one another. As I described in *The God Catchers:*

I no longer attend church meetings to minister to people; I go to minister to Him. Ever since He touched me, I go to every church meeting, worship service, and prayer gathering, saying, "I wonder if this will be the night He will show up again?"

. . . I don't know if that is where you live, but I am desperately hungry for an outbreak of God. (pp. 51–52)

I'm convinced that a true outbreak of God will affect the unsaved even more than it touches those already in the church!

PRAYER

Lord, send us a flood of Your presence that will overflow every artificial barrier, container, or wall we've constructed in the church by accident or by design. Break out in Your glory and flood the whole earth with the brilliance of Your presence. I will greet every new day and every gathering of the saints with a holy hope: "Maybe this is the time He will come."

What Have You Done with My Church?

Some of us have stuffed ourselves on spiritual junk food long enough.
There's an aching cry inside us for something more, but not for more of
man's brand of church . . . I am four generations deep in church, but I don't
know if that qualifies me for anything except to say that I don't like what I
perceive man has done with church.

THE GOD CATCHERS, P. 53

SCRIPTURE READING:

1 Corinthians 2:4–5; 4:20, where the apostle Paul declares the kingdom of
God is in power, not in word; and he preaches to establish faith in the
power of God, not in man's wisdom.

Countless Christians around the world are familiar with that aching cry
of the heart for more of God than they are finding in traditional "church as
usual" settings. Logic implies that one of three possible scenarios caused the
church of today to look and act so differently from the biblical church of
yesterday.

In the first scenario, God has changed since the days of Peter and Paul,
which explains why the church has changed. In the second scenario, held by
many modern Protestant churches, the role of the church changed after the
passing of the original apostles. In the third scenario, the church changed in
ways that removed or dismissed the presence of God and the power that
comes with it.

Has God changed? Is that even possible, according to the
Scriptures? Did the Great Commission change after the original

apostles died? Did the church cease to be a supernatural entity after the second century, or did the church change while God remained the same (as supernatural as He ever was)?

I bared my heart in the following passage from *The God Catchers*. As you read it, listen for the voice of the Spirit in your heart:

WE NEED TO SEE CHURCH AS GOD DEFINES IT

I think God's brand of church splits the heavens wide open and opens a window of glorious access between God and man. It releases such power that it starts New Testament churches and re-creates the joy, the ecstasy, and the sound and fury that the 120 experienced in the Upper Room in Jerusalem on pentecost two thousand years ago. I don't know about you, but I can't say that I've attended a meeting like that yet, and I know I'd remember it. Everyone would. (*The God Catchers,* pp. 53–54)

Is the Spirit of God confirming these words as true, or do they simply reflect Tommy Tenney's personal preferences or wishes? Do these thoughts line up with the gospel record? (You should ask yourself this question any time you read another person's writings about God's Word or His kingdom.)

When you compare the church of the first century with the church of the twenty-first century, it becomes clear that something has been lost between then and now. We don't appear to be suffering from a lack of knowledge. The Old and New Testaments are available to more people in more languages than ever before. The teachings of skilled Bible teachers and scholars over two millennia have been carefully preserved, analyzed, and summarized for those who want to tap their wisdom. The average Christian in many nations has heard more sermons and absorbed more theology than most of the early disciples received in their lifetimes.

Where is the fruit of all this knowledge? What happened to transform the church of power and spiritual passion in the first century

into the powerless and dispassionate institutions we see dotting the spiritual landscape today?

We obviously lack power and passion. Although there are a few significant exceptions to this statement, too many local churches appear to be laboring on in religious ruts powered solely by the strength of intellect, mental assent, and religious tradition. As I asserted in *The God Catchers,*

> At some point we have to say to Him, "It is You that we want." Too many of us are content with the tried and proven ways of man, where we work our way into His presence with outward shows of righteousness and a secret intention of human manipulation. (p. 54)

The only way to have a church of power is to have a life-changing encounter with the all-powerful God. The supernatural element bound in the warp and woof of the first church born on pentecost must be restored to our foundations.

Are you prepared to live and act as if God really does exist and really does intervene in the affairs of the human race? (It could cost you everything.)

PRAYER

I'm tired of displaying a powerless faith to a generation desperate to see proof of a powerful God. Lord, I want to see Your face, and then I want to return to those in darkness bearing Your light in my heart and eyes. It's power that we need, but power comes naturally when we encounter Your manifest presence, the open display of Your power and glory. Come, Lord, we are desperate for You.

Don't Do It in Spite of Us—
Do It Through Us!

God is restless to break out in this generation, and He will do it in spite of us if He has to.

THE GOD CATCHERS, P. 55

SCRIPTURE READING:

Acts 17:6, which demonstrates the power exerted by true world changers filled with passion for Christ: "These who have turned the world upside down have come here too."

Have you noticed just how odd the human race can be at times? We may relentlessly pursue the mate of our dreams until we finally claim the person as our own at the altar. Yet after the honeymoon is over, many may ask themselves when and how the fire went out. We often seem to prefer the excitement of the chase to the commitment after the catching.

Unfortunately this also seems to describe the course of the typical Christian life. Joy floods our lives when we first encounter the Lover of our souls, but once He allows us to catch Him for the first time (in truth, He purchased us with His blood), we wonder where our passion went. We've been there and done that, so now we go to church and play the religious game because we are just along for the ride.

Objectively examine the spiritual hunger level in your life in the church, and compare it with the level of spiritual hunger you see in the secular media, in the workplace, and in the shopping centers and malls in your area. Which one seems greater?

If we fail to discard our man-programs and make room for Him in our churches, then He will break out in barrooms. In fact, God shows a peculiar liking for the kind of spiritual hunger that shows up outside the buildings we think are so holy. (*The God Catchers,* p. 55)

Doesn't it seem odd that the Son of God sought out spiritual leaders from fishing villages, tax collection offices, and remote rural locations instead of checking out the best and the brightest students at the temple in Jerusalem?

Perhaps Jesus was more interested in hunger and passion than in education and religious credentials. Some of the strongest criticism He received came when He did the unthinkable—at least as far as the Pharisees were concerned. He dared to eat and fellowship with tax collectors and former prostitutes, and then He allowed them to join His motley crew of world changers.

If the Father gave you the assignment to change your world using a team that you had to select and train in just three years, what kind of recruits would you seek out? Why? How would you train them to become world changers for God? (Do you realize that this is your assignment, but without a specific timeline?)

PRAYER

Rock the world through me, not in spite of me, Lord. I surrender my will, my agenda, my plans, and even my failures to You. You chose me. Now I trust You to fill me with Your glory and plant me where You want me to bloom. Above all, I will continue to seek Your face and dwell in Your presence wherever I find myself. My life is no longer my own, for I have been bought with a price. "Spend me" to change my world and save others, Lord.

Will You Watch Him Pass By or Jump in with Him?

We can easily miss our moment of visitation if He doesn't come in the format that we think He should! (It is almost certain that He will.) There is only one way to avoid the error of the priests on the day of the triumphant entry: at some point we must get desperately hungry for Him.

THE GOD CATCHERS, P. 59

SCRIPTURE READING:

John 11:47–53, in which the chief priests and Pharisees receive an accurate prophecy from their high priest concerning the necessity of Jesus' death for the nation, and promptly begin plotting His murder themselves.

The Pharisees of Jesus' day missed their moment of visitation because they couldn't accept the fact that the Messiah didn't come to them in the manner of their own choosing. They wanted a political savior who would preserve their social stature and religious structure, but God sent a Savior to lay down His life for all races and establish a totally new kingdom and religious order.

If they were as well versed in the Old Testament Scriptures as they claimed to be, it seems they should have understood God's pattern of being totally unique, original, and very often unpredictable by human standards.

Would our pursuit of the Reviver and of revival be as difficult if we were as well versed in the Scriptures as we claim to be? Is it possible that we—the church—have missed His visitation at times by

forgetting God's pattern of being totally unique, original, and very often unpredictable?

We seem to struggle with the idea that while God never changes, He does move and change His ways of dealing with us. In our minds, a God who never changes should fit neatly into our individual theological cubbyholes and intellectual boxes.

A God who is uncontainable, uncontrollable, and unpredictable is, well, scary to minds that crave control, uniformity, security, and conventional ways of life.

The truth is that if those characteristics seem scary to human minds, then God *is* scary. He is God—fully supernatural and all-powerful and all-knowing at all times and in all places, without apology or deference to our opinions.

Have you ever experienced the manifestation of God's glory (in contrast to the presence of His anointing) in a meeting or private prayer time? Chances are that if you have, then you also experienced a new taste of the fear of God. What aspect of God's nature would inspire fear in the human heart?

Sometimes I wonder if the church is ready for God to answer its prayers, especially the prayers seeking His presence or a baptism in power. We can be certain that His answer would come swiftly and with such force that we may not even identify His presence with the weak and passive concepts of glory we've cherished for generations. The original biblical languages paint a far different picture of glory than our English translations. I described it in my book *God's Favorite House:*

In every instance where I have seen a measure of God's glory enter a worship service, a godly reverence, fear, and dread of His glory also entered the room. Even redeemed, blood-washed church leaders who lead holy lives suddenly feel a deep urgency to fall on their faces and repent before their holy God when His kabod, or weighty presence, begins to fill the room . . . This is why the earthly disciples always had to be reassured when a theophany or an angel appeared before them. They feared that the glory would kill them![15]

Could your church benefit from a dose of "godly reverence, fear, and dread of [God's] glory"? How would a visitation of God's glory change the way your church has church?

The typical religious agenda or order of service in local churches just isn't set up for an invasion of God's glory. This is why I say, "The truth is that we really have to be careful or our preselected religious agendas will make us miss what God is trying to do in this generation!" (*The God Catchers*, p. 57).

If we are not careful, we can lock ourselves inside our church traditions, agendas, programs, and empty rituals praying for Him to come while He passes by outside our religious box!

. . . Shall we just gather at the river? I say we jump in! The promised land is waiting! (*The God Catchers*, p. 59)

PRAYER

Lord, I'm tired of gathering without any swimming. Yes, I fear the fire of Your glory, but it is the heart of Your presence. I'm ready to jump in, even if it kills everything in me that did not come from You! I'm too desperate for You to hesitate any longer.

When Destiny Meets Desperation

No More Jesus Parades

Desperation brings a certain purifying element to our relationships with God. In the heat of crisis or hunger, we finally abandon our habitual pretense and religious posturing to cry out from the heart rather than the mind.

Based on God's comment to the church of Laodicea ("because you are lukewarm, and neither cold nor hot, I will vomit you out of My mouth"),[1] it almost seems that God would rather deal with a cursing but honest sinner than with the flattery of an apathetic and hypocritical spectator Christian.

The Scriptures and human experience agree: a supernatural transaction takes place in the human soul when divine destiny meets human desperation in His presence.

It's Better to Be a Hungry Baby than a Stuffed and Complacent "Maybe"

[God] has noticed that the repetitive falsehoods are fading away, and He's waiting for them to be replaced by a new vocabulary of honesty: "No, I am not all right, and everything isn't fine—I'm hungry!"

THE GOD CATCHERS, P. 63

SCRIPTURE READING:

Matthew 11:28–30, in which Jesus calls to Himself everyone who is weary and overloaded.

On rare occasions, instinctive human behavior appears to faintly resemble divine behavior. For instance, when was the last time you saw a flock of adults rush toward another adult to coo, ooh, and ah, and make a big fuss over him? When was the last time you saw this happen when a little baby was brought into a room?

Is it wrong to imply that Christians should remain babies in some way? Is it possible or desirable to somehow "grow up" in Christ while retaining a baby's total dependence and crying need for Him? (Are you interested?)

Perhaps you noticed that there is something about childlike dependency, trust, and urgent need in the human heart that captures the heart of Divinity. Jesus had His "little ones" in mind when He issued some of the New Testament's strongest and most severe warnings about misuse and abuse.[2] He was talking about more than natural babies and toddlers; He was referring to everyone, young and old, who cries out to Him with juvenile cries of desperation and dependency.

Are you convinced that His words apply to you? Why or why not?

God loves us all without showing partiality, but He does extend the extra care and protection found in His presence to those who openly demonstrate their urgent need for Him.

> Hungry babies just aren't intimidated by the people around them. They put their total focus and energy on their hunger and the source of their satisfaction. At the height of their hunger, they make no room for distractions of any kind. (*The God Catchers,* p. 62)

In contrast, many Christians do their best to demonstrate their independence and self-sufficiency in public worship gatherings. They would never think of going forward in a public invitation for prayer. Such a transparent admission of need is unacceptable because it would reveal politically incorrect cracks in their carefully cultivated facade of Christian perfection. In their determined effort not to attract any attention to their need, they've also managed to totally lose God's interest and attention!

Where do you fit in this picture? Are you a bold and hungry baby in His presence or a stuffed and complacent "maybe" who approaches worship on a whim, willing to worship Him as long as you feel like it?

> Some of us have "faked fullness" for most of our Christian lives. Whether in church or on the job, we live with a pasted-on smile, and we refuse to leave home without it. The truth is that more and more Christian "fakers of fullness" are saying, "I've had enough of that." Their inner hunger is beginning to get the best of them, and God is beginning to get interested once again. (*The God Catchers,* p. 63)

Have you had enough? Is your inner hunger level beginning to get the best of you?

PRAYER

Lord, I'm so hungry for You that I've dropped every facade of fakery I possessed. I don't care who knows how desperate I am. I need You!

Let Hunger Rise and Have Its Say!

Have we become like the Laodicean church members who said, "I am rich, have become wealthy, and have need of nothing," while totally unaware that they were "wretched, miserable, poor, blind, and naked"?[3]

THE GOD CATCHERS, P. 63

SCRIPTURE READING:

Revelation 3:14–19, in which Jesus reveals the desperate condition of the complacent and satisfied church.

Rent a meeting room, set tables, and invite two hundred guests to a five-course meal fit for kings. Then watch what happens when your guests are served by perfectly dressed and trained waiters delivering single servings of sugar pills, pieces of fruit-flavored chewing gum on toothpicks, breath mints, antacid tablets, and plastic-wrapped candies. The guests may manage to preserve the pretense of civility for one or two of these "courses," but the time inevitably will come when someone brave enough to break the silence will voice his hunger (and irritation with such a facade of a feast).

Would this one person's honesty make his less vocal companions feel embarrassed at first? Would that make his honesty inappropriate or wrong? How does this example apply to your life and your local church experience?

The medical world uses the term "placebos" to describe the sugar pills that physicians sometimes prescribe as "medications" for unknowing patients.

These "medications" have no medicinal or nutritional properties, but the patients gladly receive them as the cure for what ails them. How many times do we go home after our worship gatherings happily clutching powerless spiritual placebos prescribed in place of the real cure for our gnawing hunger of the heart? (It is rare to find an insincere or dishonest pastor, so the problem must be that spiritual leaders are simply human too.)

We go through life trying to fill our existence with empty platitudes and man-pleasing programs while we gradually grow weaker and colder in spirit—until the day hunger finally rises up to have its say.

Have you ever felt desire rise up in your soul to voice your hunger in desperate tones? What would happen when or if it did?

Why does it take so long for us to perceive our condition and seek the face of our Cure? In the absence of courage, truth is most often concealed and weakness is rarely revealed. God had good reason to warn us that fearing man is the equivalent of a dangerous trap set for our souls.[4] Momentary fear races through entire church congregations when even one voice rises to God in uninhibited frustration and desperation, saying, "God, I need You!"

When this kind of honesty surfaces in a church service, we start to feel awkward. That is because most of us are uncomfortable with this amount of intense hunger . . .

We are afraid to recognize and confess our gnawing hunger of the heart, and we are even more afraid of its cure—a fresh and intimate encounter with the presence of God. It's simple: God's children need more than Daddy's Word, Daddy's gifts, Daddy's daily provision, or the assistance of Daddy's earthly assistants. We need Him. We desperately long to feel His touch on our lives. (*The God Catchers*, pp. 63–64)

Why would God release such a spirit of hunger in a local church? Why did He put this book in your hands? Could it be that desperate hunger is part of His divine agenda for you?

PRAYER

Father, not my will but Yours be done. In Your mercy, deliver me from the snare of satisfaction and the sin of complacency. Thank You for opening my eyes to my desperate condition. I'm determined to pursue You and soothe my heart's longing in Your presence.

Climb God's Tree of Sovereignty to Activate Your Destiny

Don't miss your moment in the Son; *God has invested more than you know in you and your encounter with Him.*

THE GOD CATCHERS, P. 65

SCRIPTURE READING:

Revelation 3:20 and 1 Samuel 3:10–11, where we learn that Jesus Christ knocks on the door of our hearts as Christians; and we consider the way young Samuel answered the knock of Divinity in his life.

Have you ever read that the God you serve "[declares] the end from the beginning"?[5] Curiosity led me to dig deeper, and that is how I discovered that the Hebrew word translated "declares" actually means "to stand boldly out opposite."[6] I don't claim to be a theologian, linguist, or English professor, but that string of words sure sounds to me like "seeing and doing things backward from the usual." That perfectly matches the situation described on page 64 of *The God Catchers:*

> Zacchaeus's friends, along with many contemporary folks who casually peruse the pages of the Bible, probably share the same thought about him: *Lucky for him that sycamore tree was there.* I am reminded that it takes longer to grow a sycamore tree than it does to grow a man, and it seems to me that our sovereign God approaches neither task lightly, casually, or haphazardly.
>
> Long before Zacchaeus was born, I believe God planted a seed beside the Jericho road.

Review your life and answer this question: What seed did God plant in the earth in anticipation of your birth—and the day you would pass His tree of destiny with a strangely compelling urge to climb it? Did you climb or decline? (You may be standing in the shade of yet another tree this very moment.)

We can count on God to "stand boldly out opposite" from our way of seeing and doing things. Man may call it lucky, but I can almost hear God's reply to us: "There was no luck involved. I work with the dynamic of destiny birthed in a meeting of divine sovereignty and human desperation." We shouldn't be surprised. God warned us that His ways and thoughts are higher than ours.[7]

"No, nothing is more important to Me than preplanning encounters with My children." Then He added, "I can't make Zacchaeus climb the tree, but I can plant the tree. Only his hunger will cause him to climb the tree. In the meantime, My sovereignty will make sure the tree is in its place, ready and waiting for his climb to destiny." (*The God Catchers,* p. 65)

If it is true that God preplans encounters with His children (and the life experiences of Adam, Noah, Abraham, Isaac, Jacob, Moses, Joshua, Samuel, Ruth, and all of the prophets along with the twelve disciples and Paul seem to confirm it), then shouldn't we make destiny tree climbing one of our prime priorities?

Isn't this just another name for God Chasing? Are you pursuing His presence or just watching the chase from the safety of a church pew or easy chair?

PRAYER

If I have to climb every tree and open every door that presents itself in my pursuit of Your face, I'll do it, Lord. I am too desperate for You to miss my moment in the presence of the Son. The cost of missing You is far higher than the cost of chasing and catching You!

Deity Over Dignity!
Accept Your Blind Date with Destiny

While Zacchaeus stood in the shadow of the sycamore tree debating over his dignity, the angels were cheering, "Go on; climb the tree, man! Get up there; we didn't guard this tree for fifty years for nothing. Deity over dignity!"

<small>THE GOD CATCHERS, P. 66</small>

SCRIPTURE READING:

Psalm 139:13–16 and John 10:10, where we see that the same God who saw us even before our conception orchestrated the birth, life, and death of His Son to give us life, that we may have it "more abundantly."

Consider this fantastic possibility: even before your conception years ago, God had already prepared and preplanned your blind date with destiny—not only in the all-important matter of salvation through Christ, but also in the fulfillment of His purposes for your life. The problem comes with human distorted concepts of personal dignity. It is possible that one Jericho tax official in particular wrestled long and hard with the crucial question of dignity:

No, someone of my stature in the community doesn't climb trees for anyone. Well, the truth is that someone of my stature will never see Him unless he climbs this tree. I'm really desperate, but how do I preserve my dignity? (*The God Catchers,* p. 66)

How often have you wrestled with dignity's indignity over the necessity of humility in the chase? No one can escape it. Have you

ever read that even Jesus "humbled Himself"?[8] Is a still small voice pressing the point of eternity in your heart? Can you hear the cry "Deity over dignity"?

After all the sovereign preparations for this blind date with destiny, this was no time for Zacchaeus to wrestle with his fear of public disapproval by a public that already disapproved of him. (*The God Catchers*, p. 66)

The Bible tells us that God shows no favoritism. He has made preparations for your blind date too. Whether or not you "wrestle" under the tree is up to you. Destiny awaits you if you climb it.

PRAYER

Lord, I would rather die with Your deity in my sight than live with man-fearing, man-pleasing dignity ruling my life. Deliver me from my dignity that I might be caught up, lifted up, transformed, and consumed in Your deity.

Too Hungry to Be Satisfied with "the Usual"

Something happened to me after decades of serving God and preaching what I thought was revival. Something was missing, and I had an idea it was God's presence. That was when I decided that I was tired of standing on the sidewalk watching the "Jesus parade" pass by. I became too hungry to be satisfied with church as usual.

THE GOD CATCHERS, P. 67

SCRIPTURE READING:

Luke 19:1–10, in which a wealthy but unpopular senior tax agent of short stature climbs a tree of destiny and becomes an unforgettable trophy of Christ's triumph, who came "to seek and to save that which was lost."

Children recognized Him instantly, and so did the adults in some great need or desperation. It was only among the smug, the satisfied, and the supposedly secure that Jesus found wholesale rejection. The wealthy tax man of Jericho had every natural need and most of the wants that are so easily supplied by money. Yet he needed something no amount of money or earthly power could purchase, control, or extort from others. Zacchaeus needed an encounter with Deity, and God sensed the desperation and determination in his soul.

Have you ever read the account of Zacchaeus or some other Bible character and then felt pangs of longing or even jealousy wracking your soul? "Why couldn't it have been me, Lord?"

The tree of Zacchaeus was the proverbial sycamore tree of divine purpose.

When humanity fell short of the glory of God, He planted another tree of inestimable worth. The tree of destiny for the rest of us was planted on the top of Calvary, and God Himself climbed it first so it would still be standing on our day of destiny. We can't see Him from any other vantage point, but if we can just climb that tree, we'll transcend time and access His abiding presence for eternity. (*The God Catchers,* pp. 66–67)

God Chasers perpetually carry a tree of destiny with them, and that tree is indivisible from true discipleship and daily obedience to Christ's call. I read somewhere, "If anyone desires to come after Me, let him deny himself, and take up his cross daily, and follow Me."[9]

Whether we like it or not, the cross of daily crucifixion and all-out commitment is mandatory for God Chasers who are too hungry to be content with church as usual.

How does the idea of daily cross bearing and God Chasing match up with our modern concept that being a Christian is mostly a matter of regular church attendance? How does it match up with your daily life?

Zacchaeus climbed the tree, but Jesus invited Himself to the house. *God plants the tree in your life, but hunger makes you climb it.* God creates the occasion, but you must take advantage of it: "Seek the LORD while He may be found, call upon Him while He is near."[10] If you dare to climb the tree of hunger, you may not have to invite Him—*He may just invite Himself.* (*The God Catchers,* p. 72)

PRAYER

Lord, I know You planted this tree of daily death to pride and dignity in my life. Part of me doesn't want to touch it, but the hungry part of my soul has forced the issue. I can't stand to wait any longer. I'm climbing that tree. I refuse to allow my fears or satisfaction with comfort to separate me from Your perfect will any longer. I'm committing to a life of perpetual pursuit— as long as You are the Pursued.

Passion for God Often Offends Men

Bartimaeus's friends couldn't do for him what Jesus could. They were offended by the beggar's cries because they perceived the cries to be distracting; but the Son of God was attracted to Bartimaeus's cries because He perceived them to be worship served on a platter of pure passion.

THE GOD CATCHERS, P. 69

SCRIPTURE READING:

Mark 10:46–52, in which blind Bartimaeus releases such passionate cries of desperation that he captures the Lord's attention over the noise and chaos of a surging crowd.

It is inevitable. The moment desperation shows up in your life, certain friends will show up with "wise counsel" designed to quench the fire, lessen the urgency, and dampen the passion—all for your own good, of course.

Even Jesus had His earthly family show up at the door asking for Him while He was still speaking.[11] Many believe they were on a mission to bring Him to His senses. If that really was their goal, He would have none of it. He was possessed with zeal for the Father and His Father's house, and He would permit no interference with His pursuit of His destiny.

Have you chased God long enough and passionately enough to offend some of your friends and loved ones? Was God offended by the passion of your pursuit?

Are you, like Bartimaeus, saying to yourself, "If I could just know for sure"? Bartimaeus didn't know for sure, but he was determined not to miss his moment. He thought, *Well, if He's this close, I have to do something to capture His attention.*

. . . If Bartimaeus had listened to his friends, he would have missed his divine appointment. One cry wasn't enough. Most of us don't like living in the tension between the first cry and God's final response. (*The God Catchers*, pp. 68–69)

Bartimaeus discovered something unpleasant and difficult in the gap of time between his first frantic cry and Jesus' final response—the tense time of waiting, uncertainty, persecution, and sheer faith experienced by everyone seeking His visitation. The first thing produced by a cry of desperation is rarely inspiration. It is usually the irritated shouts, comments, or whispers of disapproving people around you. As I explained in *The God Catchers*, "If the first voice that reaches you after your first cry of hunger says, 'Calm down,' it probably won't be the voice of God" (p. 69).

Have you heard conflicting voices speak to you since you began the chase? Did the first voices urge you on in your passionate pursuit of Deity, or did they pressure you to maintain the proper posture of humanity at rest?

PRAYER

I'm determined not to miss my moment with You, Lord. If You're this close, I have to do something to capture Your attention! I'm desperate for You: "Jesus, Son of David, have mercy on me!"[12]

Desperate Enough
to Arrest God's Attention

I wish more of us in the church would get tired of standing on the sidewalk of spectator Christianity while the "Jesus parade" goes by. Somebody needs to get hungry enough to cry out. Somebody needs to get desperate enough to arrest the attention of heaven and say, "I'm not going to let You pass me by, Lord. I thank You for what You have done, but I'm desperate for what You can do."

THE GOD CATCHERS, P. 72

SCRIPTURE READING:

Matthew 15:22–28, where the widow from Canaan arrests the attention of Jesus and receives a miracle through persistent and passionate faith.

Most people have a persistent picture of Jesus Christ reaching out to people who are blind, demonized, or physically disabled. There isn't anything wrong with this picture because He does come to us. We know from the Scriptures that we love Him because He loved us first.[13] The problem arises when you let this one-dimensional view limit your response to Him. The fact is that really desperate people often reach out to Him using every means available.

What picture of the Master hangs in the wall of your memory? Is He coming to you or to others in need, or are you running to Him? Do you unconsciously expect Him to always come to you in times of need, or do you understand your responsibility to run to Him as well?

98

Bartimaeus cried out to Jesus with all of the power his lungs could muster.[14]

The woman suffering from an incurable and chronic blood hemorrhage pursued Him in the middle of a crushing crowd. She risked everything just to secretly touch the hem of His garment, which may indicate that she approached Jesus from behind on her hands and knees while using one hand to fend away the feet of the crowd pressing around and above her.[15]

The persistent mother from Canaan pursued Him beyond the accepted boundaries of social, racial, and religious protocols. She was desperate to win deliverance for her daughter.[16]

The demoniac possessed by a legion of demons rushed to meet Jesus at the lakeshore with his body covered by nothing but the blood from his self-mutilation.[17]

The desperate friends of the paralyzed man who spent his days and nights on a litter resorted to property damage and breaking and entering to place him in the presence of the Healer.[18]

It is sobering to realize that none of these responses would be considered acceptable in the typical North American church service! (The ushers would have those nuisances out the door before the second offering.) I long for the day it is not only acceptable but also common for the lost and hurting to cry out and run to Him in our worship services.

If these responses were acceptable to Jesus Christ, why would they be unacceptable in churches today? What would you do if you knew you had to capture the attention of God in some way?

Bartimaeus couldn't even see the One he was chasing. He was incapable of effectively pursuing Jesus in a physical way, yet the blind beggar became the God Catcher that day. How did he do it?

. . . What did Bartimaeus do to arrest the momentum of the Messiah? Examine the words he sent from his heart to the ears of God. He said, "Jesus, Son of David, have mercy on me!" He worshiped! With all the passion, hunger, and desperation in his being, the son of Timaeus arrested the attention of the Son of God. Radical praise brings radical presence! (*The God Catchers*, pp. 70–71)

PRAYER

Lord, I don't want to be presumptuous, and I don't want to be too proud to cry out to You either. All I know is that I need You more than I need the approval and blessings of anyone else. I love my family and friends, but they can't give me what You can—the privilege of dwelling in Your presence. If I'm desperate enough to cry out to You, then maybe I can arrest Your attention and catch You once more with my passionate worship.

What Does a Human Waiter Offer a Divine Customer?

Waiting in Café Heaven Is Not Spiritual Thumb Twiddling

Just a few years ago, most of us would have scoffed at the idea that we are waiters in some celestial diner, carefully waiting for Divinity's selection from some pitiful menu of humanity. Yet God is patiently teaching us how to be good waiters.

As inconceivable as it may seem, there is something on our pitiful menu that attracts God's presence to our humble serving table, and it has virtually nothing to do with the usual fare that we serve in our services.

He has no appetite for good preaching or even good offerings, although He fully expects to find these things in the house (these things are for us, just as good employee training, health insurance, and a retirement plan are often the marks of a good restaurant).

God is after something prepared only for Him. When they choose to devote themselves to it, humanity's chefs are unequaled in their preparation and service of His favorite cuisine.

He Is the Cure for Our "Me" Disease

A lot of Christians never "get it." . . . They think church is about them, so they turn church into glorified "bless me clubs" when God thinks it's a "bless Him club." God has this incredible idea that church is all about Him, and He can't seem to get it out of His mind.

THE GOD CATCHERS, P. 76

SCRIPTURE READING:

Romans 8:10–14, where Paul clearly says we must "put to death the deeds of the body" and be led by the Spirit.

Two of the most persistent and destructive deeds of the flesh include our human tendency to claim God's glory as our own and our stubborn habit of steering our worship services closer to man's heart than to God's. In *The God Catchers*, I commented,

> For some reason, God actually thinks people dress up and gather together in a church meeting for Him! That gives new meaning to the phrase, "waiting on the Lord," doesn't it? (p. 77)

Have you noticed that things we do in church are generally considered exempt from our thinking about "deeds of the flesh"? Examine a typical church service and contrast the things that might please God with the things that would please only the flesh.

Few people have the time or patience to pity what I called "pretend waiters" in *The God Catchers*. It is almost certain that you have suffered at the hands of these pretenders who feel obligated to interrupt your meal and conversations

102

every five minutes or so, even in some of the finest restaurants. I wonder how God classifies the quality and consideration of our waiting in the spiritual restaurant called the church?

How would you rate your waiting skills? Who ranks first on your "ones to please" list each day and especially in corporate worship settings?

I've noticed that whenever God begins to manifest His presence in our services, we have to suspend our plans. At that touchy point of self-sacrifice many of us resent His visitation as an inconvenience! Though we may never say it out loud, something in us may think, *How dare He interrupt our carefully devised plans—He almost acts as if He owns that place.*

Have you ever felt irritation and offense over God's interruption of your plans? Did you turn your back on the supposed offense or on the alleged Offender? Are you willing to embrace some temporal disappointment in exchange for divine visitation?

In *The God Catchers*, you read,

The Lord loves to come to services where we anticipate His every desire and whim. He delights to see us carefully seek the guidance of the Holy Spirit in every part of the service—whether our preset song lists, order of service, or programs are disrupted or not. (p. 78)

He is the cure for our "me" disease, but it all begins with us. We possess the power to change the level and quality of service in our worship services. God is ready and willing to manifest His glory among us. It is up to us now.

PRAYER

May my interrupting days be over, Lord. You are my main focus, my first desire, and my Primary Customer. I'm so desperate for Your presence that I'll sacrifice all of my personal agendas, plans, and protocols on the altar just for another moment in Your manifest presence. Please forgive me for all of the times I've interrupted Your visitation to preserve my implementation of merely human plans and purposes. You are my first love. Now I will put You in first place.

Are You Seated High Enough to See What Was Always There?

If we forget that this is all about Him, if we revert to the myth that church is all about us, then we never quite enter in and we miss the whole purpose of it all. The short version of this is that we need a perspective change.

THE GOD CATCHERS, P. 79

SCRIPTURE READING:

Colossians 3:1–3 and 2 Peter 1:3–4, where Paul commands us to seek the things above and set our affections above; where Christ sits at the right hand of God; and where Peter assures us that God has already given us everything we need for success in this life.

In the moments when our vision is the clearest, we readily admit that most of our lives are spent on us and not on Him. We may even admit that much of the time we invest in corporate worship is devoted to our issues and not His. God really doesn't mind our dealing with our issues in church; He cares about every detail of our lives. However, I think He wonders when we will return to our first priority and purpose in life—loving and pleasing Him.

Has the myth of "us" stolen the promise of His presence in your local church services? Is it time for a personal and corporate perspective change to refocus the service on Him?

We aren't as smug or self-centered when we devote more attention to Him than to us during our worship services. Why? We can't march according to human maps and man-made priorities in those meetings. We have no choice but to search for and seek out the face of the God, who has the habit of moving on us to keep us out of presumption and habitual ritual. Any commitment to finding this God who hides can create a measure of godly tension and discomfort at times.

> It's a lot like trying to find the opening in heavy, room-darkening shades in an unfamiliar hotel room in the morning. Some of those rooms can get so dark that you can't tell what time of day it is. Sometimes you get out of bed and try to find the opening in the drapes by running your fingers along the pleats until you suddenly see a shaft of light. "Oh, there it is."
>
> That is what we do in our services sometimes. We don't exactly know where the opening leading to His presence is, so we just run our hands along the pleats of the veil until we find the place where it has been freshly ripped.[1]

Are you committed to finding the God who hides? Just how uncomfortable and stretched are you willing to become in your pursuit of His presence?

God tends to take us beyond the edge of our comfort zones to change our perspective of His presence. He will gladly disrupt the patterns of entire congregations and cities if it means He will be welcomed and served with His favorite delight in the end. It all comes back to the question, What does a human waiter offer a divine customer? (Add the question, What is the human waiter prepared to sacrifice for Divinity's pleasure?)

PRAYER

Lord, forgive me for setting my sights on things that are low and lifting them up instead of raising them to view You, high and lifted up. I am hungry for You, and now I see that the only way to experience Your manifest presence is to wait upon You and put Your desire for true worship first. I'm determined to wait upon You and pursue You until I find You.

What Spirit Possesses You to Sing at Midnight?

Your heavenly Father never intended for you to dwell in the earthly realm, constantly looking at and dwelling on your problems. You were birthed for the heavenlies. In fact, you are the only creature of earth that was birthed for the heavenlies. Everything else in the earthly realm must stay in this realm. You don't belong down here, so shake off those earthly chains!

THE GOD CATCHERS, P. 81

SCRIPTURE READING:

Ephesians 2:4–7, where Paul tells us we have been raised up together with Christ and are seated with Him in heavenly places.

It seems backward somehow, but the best way to make things better when we feel bad is to worship God. Naturally the last thing our flesh wants to do when things are bad is to thank God for His blessings and worship Him. It may not make much sense to the human mind, but it makes perfect sense in the mind of Deity.

What is your natural response when things go bad in your life? Do you want to run away from the problems, run to God and cry for help, or drop to your knees and worship Him? Which choice seems most logical?

Consider the illogical actions of Paul and Silas in Acts 16. The prisoners chained to the walls and locked in the stocks of the ancient Philippian prison in Macedonia probably thought the two men held in the inner dungeon were out of their minds. It is likely the old-timers in that place had never heard sane men sing in that foul-smelling darkness, yet those two newcomers were singing and worshiping their God so loudly, their voices were hoarse!

The diagnosis of insanity was even more probable since everyone in the prison heard the sickening *thunk* of rods striking human flesh just before the strangers were brought to the cell reserved for chief offenders. As midnight approached, the prisoners listened to the singing and thought, *What unearthly spirit possesses these men and causes them to sing and pray when they should be wailing in pain and cursing the men who beat them?*

What spirit possesses you in times of pain, difficulty, or impossibility? Do you sing and pray to Him or moan and groan to men in the midnight hour of adversity?

What is the secret of worship during the dark hours of life?

When you begin to worship, you ascend to join the Object of your adoration. The Bible says God "made us sit together in the heavenly places in Christ Jesus." (*The God Catchers,* p. 81)

There is no evidence that our divine seating assignment changes with changing circumstances on earth, and there is a certain logic to the idea that when you have a big problem, you should seek out a bigger solution.

When you have an encounter with the presence of God, the problems that loomed so large that they blocked out the light of hope itself suddenly seem to be so much smaller that they've lost their power to paralyze and control your life. Did the problems change? No. Your perspective changed. You now view them from the eternal perspective of heaven as God always intended.

That is what worship does for you. Your problems aren't too big—perhaps your worship is too small![2]

PRAYER

Worship is my lifestyle, Lord. I won't reserve it for the comfort of an organized worship service with other believers. I'll also tap its deep well in the dark hours of my life. The demand for worship is as constant as the faithfulness of Your love and the depth of Your worth as the almighty Creator. Therefore, I will praise You in good times and bad, and I will worship You morning, noon, and night, Lord. I'm desperate for You, and in You I have everything I need.

The Proof Is in the Waiting

Everybody likes the end results of a miracle, but no one likes the waiting process. Yet it is in the waiting that He actually proves He is God in response to your absolute dependency on Him. Waiting puts you in the position to know that Satan cannot rob you, and that it is impossible for God to be "late."

THE GOD CATCHERS, P. 86

SCRIPTURE READING:

Psalm 27:11–14, in which David urges us to wait patiently before the Lord.

David clearly understood the concept of waiting on God. He didn't offer us theory, conjecture, or imagination when he wrote about waiting in the Psalms. He had impeccable credentials as a waiter.

The prophet Samuel anointed David as Israel's new king when he was still a youth, but David didn't assume the throne until he was thirty years old.[3] In fact, he spent most of those years waiting on God while running for his life from King Saul. He waited, worshiped, cried out, and praised God in caves, in the cities of his enemies, and in the wilderness. Later, King David even waited on God when his own son rebelled, assumed the throne, and led an army campaign to murder him. The proof of God's presence in David's life was in the waiting, and in the results produced by his waiting on Deity.

Which part of David's life do you prefer: the promise part, the waiting part, or the ruling part? Which part of your life do you prefer? Which is the most important?

The only way we can "entertain" God's presence is by waiting on Him. If we want His presence to invade our individual lives, we must learn to wait on Him individually. If we long to see His presence invade our churches or our city, then we must learn to wait on Him and serve Him in corporate unity. Remember that you must deal with first things first. Become a good waiter privately before you can effectively play a role corporately.

How are your personal waiting skills? Do you know how to make God feel at home in your home?

In most cases, we could maintain life and church as usual even if God never showed up. That means we have little or no true dependency upon Him. He proves He is God as we wait upon Him in absolute dependency.

Any way you look at it, we must restructure our lives and worship to restore true dependence on Deity and less dependence on humanity.

Prayer

Father, I've been living far too independently lately. I renounce every independence in my life, and I announce my total and complete dependence upon You. I am completely and permanently in need of Your presence moment by moment. Apart from You I can do nothing but fail and fall. I will patiently wait on You: hungry, thirsty, and longing for Your presence.

God Chasers Never Play with Man's Matches!

Our problem is that we get in such an all-fired hurry to get results that we try to use man's matches to set our own hair on fire! There is a big difference between the fire of God and the fire of man.

THE GOD CATCHERS, P. 90

SCRIPTURE READING:

Leviticus 10:1–3; Luke 24:49; and Acts 2, which contrast the strange or profane fire of man with the fire of God experienced by the 120 at pentecost.

Every year, a number of weekend barbecue fans and cookout kings experience close calls with eternity and the emergency room when they grow impatient with their stubborn charcoal fires. "Let's hurry this thing up," they say. After they "anoint" their burned sacrifice with highly flammable gasoline or charcoal lighter fluid, they light a man-made match that nearly ends life as they know it.

Two sons of Aaron tried to hurry up their priestly service to God by introducing "profane fire" into God's holy presence, and they became the barbecue that day.[4] In the spiritual realm, God's fire and man's matches don't mix at all, but we ignore the warnings and wonder why we get burned so often in our quest for revival fire. True revival can come only from the true Reviver. No substitute will do.

Have you or a church leader you know ever grown so impatient with the chase that efforts were made to hurry up God by using one of man's matches (such as booking a surefire evangelist, using

112

revival formulas, or implementing "fire in the church" programs)? Did any of them really work?

Patient waiting and service are indispensable tools for true God Chasers. In a sense, the pursuit of God's presence is similar to the natural process of pregnancy and delivery. Without the waiting there is no delivery. If delivery comes before its time or is artificially triggered by a foreign substance, then there is a serious risk of spontaneous abortion or miscarriage.

The actual birthing stage of the pregnancy process usually comes to a climax in a matter of hours or a day at most, but it takes nine months of waiting to reach that point. Mothers who have carried a baby from conception to birth understand the sweet pain of waiting. (*The God Catchers,* p. 89)

Do you understand the "sweet pain of waiting" for His presence? Is the joy of His arrival worth the pain of the wait?

Jesus told the disciples to "tarry" or patiently wait on the arrival of God's fire in the person of the Holy Spirit. They followed His instructions without question, not by twiddling their thumbs. They waited and served God in prayer and unity until the time of divine delivery arrived. I was surprised to see that A. B. Bruce, a biblical scholar of the nineteenth century, described the delivery this way in his classic theological work, *The Training of the Twelve:* "The events of Pentecost were the answer to the prayers offered up during those ten days, which we may call the incubation period of the Christian Church."[5]

Waiting, tarrying, pregnancy, incubation—all of these words speak of patience, endurance, and eager anticipation of something more and greater coming our way. The bottom line is this: God Chasers never play with man's matches, no matter how impatient we may feel. There simply is no substitute for the Real Thing, and God's presence comes when, how, and where God chooses. All we can do is wait.

Is it easier to wait, knowing that it is a natural part of God's plan for your pursuit of His presence? How does it change your perspective of the dry periods you face as a God Chaser?

PRAYER

Lord, I feel pregnant with Your purposes. Labor has overtaken me, and desire for the arrival of Your presence moves me to press on and press in. Lord, I will wait upon You as long as it takes.

Never Interrupt God's Disruptions

Sometimes our greatest temptations for interrupting God's divine disruptions are rooted in some of God's best gifts.

THE GOD CATCHERS, P. 91

SCRIPTURE READING:

Matthew 6:25–33, where Jesus gives us the prescription for stress relief and proper focus in every area of life (which includes the balance between seeking God and seeking His provision).

At every Christmas season and at every birthday, children in North America face a crucial test unawares—a test that may prepare them for effective service in the family of God. What do they do when their parents give them good gifts on those special occasions? Do they take time to look Mom and Dad in the eye and thank them before rushing off to play with their gifts in another room? Do they climb up in their laps and give them snug hugs of gratitude and love, or do they rip off the wrapping paper and disappear without so much as a "Thanks, bye, see you later"?

Did you pass the test in your youth? Did you pass the test the last time you encountered Him in a corporate worship service or prayer meeting?

Our Father in heaven has blessed us abundantly, but all too often we get caught up in the rushed pace of life and quickly go our way, much as the nine men with leprosy who failed to return and praise God after Jesus healed them. Sometimes I wonder whether Jesus is still saying, "Were there not any found who returned to give glory to God except this foreigner?"[6]

Some of His best gifts include His spiritual gifts,[7] the spiritually gifted people He sends to lead and equip the church,[8] and His inspired Word. The problem is that we tend to grab His gifts and hole away in our rooms playing church games while forgetting about Him.

We are so *blessed* by God's Word and by His leaders and charismatic gifts that we can quickly forget that church is about Him, not us. He gave us these gifts to equip us, heal us, lead us, confront us, strengthen us, instruct us, enlighten us, and inspire us in our Christian walk. However, God's gifts should never, ever, in no way whatsoever, take away or minimize our service of love to Him. Our primary object of pursuit should be the Giver, not the gifts![9]

How easily are you distracted from your primary pursuit of the Giver by the splendid quality of His abundant gifts to you and to the church body? How do you reset your focus when this happens?

Far too often, God's people place their affections on the blessings and gifts God gives them to meet their personal needs. He delights in giving good gifts to His children, but His chief delight is in receiving love, adoration, and worship directly from them. It all boils down to who wants to give more than receive.

On the occasions when we seek His face rather than His hands, He inevitably meets us in the face place of worship. Yet the moment we sense His manifest presence, we often abandon our position of worship to assume the position of petition, turning our focus from the face of the Giver to His hands. At other times, as soon as His manifest presence raises our excitement level, we want to interrupt our visit with Him to take His gifts and meet the needs of humanity. That isn't a bad thing, but in comparison to ministering to Him, it isn't the best thing. Once we minister to Him, we will find it far easier to minister to man's needs with unequaled authority and spiritual power.

These are not deadly sins or unforgivable mistakes, but they usually cut short our visit with Deity. His manifest presence usually lifts so we can continue our ministry to one another without any further interruption from Deity.

Have you experienced any of these "interruptions of God's disruptions" in your life or in a meeting? What happened when you turned your eyes from His face to minister in His place?

Perhaps I said it best in *The God Catchers:*

You know men are reaching in their own pockets for matches when their words indicate the presence of a fleshly clock somewhere:

"Is this service going somewhere? We need to do something. I just wish we'd hurry up and get to the point."

He is the point. His presence is the destination.

"Well, what are we going to do? What's next?"

That is like standing on top of Mount Everest and saying, "Which way is up?" One step in any direction is a step down. (p. 90)

PRAYER

The truth is that I've lived with less than the best all of my life, Lord. Now that I've discovered the wonder of Your presence, I'm ruined for second best. Now that I've discovered there is more of You for the asking and the chasing, I live for each new moment of divine encounter. One step in any direction is a step down, and I refuse to take that plunge. My heart longs for You, and nothing and no one less will do.

What Does a Human Waiter Offer a Divine Customer?

If you have made a good beginning, do not let the pregnancy of purpose turn into a miscarriage of man or an abortion. God is tired of tapping a shoulder in vain attempts to wrestle us away from our agendas, religious ruts, and fleshly formulas for church. He's looking for a radical few who will say, "I'm going to wait on You until it all happens."

THE GOD CATCHERS, P. 94

SCRIPTURE READING:

Philippians 3:12–14, where Paul describes his all-or-nothing approach to God Chasing and being apprehended by God (or what we call God Catching).

So what does a human waiter offer a divine customer? "You offer Him good 'service'! Offer Him persistent worship and insistent hunger that refuse to give up until He shows up, not spiritual thumb twiddling!" (*The God Catchers*, p. 94).

Virtually anything that is labeled "persistent" or "insistent" is discarded by passive religious systems as presumptuous toward God or as too works-oriented. Evidently somebody forgot to tell Jesus that because He "mistakenly" brought it up in His ministry.

How do you view people who are persistent or insistent in their comments, complaints, or requests to you? Have you ever approached God with a persistent or insistent heart (in line with His Word, of course)?

Jesus specifically told His disciples to pray like the widow who knocked on the judge's door so persistently that he finally granted her request just to get rid of her irritating insistence.[10] There is no evidence that Jesus made a mistake here, or anywhere else for that matter, but we like to act as if it were a mistake. On the contrary, Jesus wanted to teach the disciples "that men always ought to pray and not lose heart."[11]

If waiting on God actually involves waiting, then do you understand why persistence and patience are so important to God Chasers who seek to become God Catchers?

Moses used the posture of worship in the battle with the Amalekites (see *The God Catchers*, p. 94). Worship is the main course a true waiter serves a divine customer. Yet there are times when you must serve Him worship in less than pleasant circumstances. True waiting comes in when you learn how to worship over your negative circumstances.

If you are a mother missing her prodigal son, then go home to that empty bed where your wayward son used to sleep. Stretch out your hands and worship over the place of opposition. Turn his empty bed into an altar and turn the tables on the adversary. Turn your health challenges into a place of worship. Turn your empty financial barns into a place of seed-sowing worship![12]

Are you facing an impossible situation, a heart wound that just won't heal, or a situation involving an enemy who is determined to stop or destroy you? Make it into a place of worship, an altar of adoration where you offer worship and praise to the God of your salvation.

Can you sense your passion breaking out of its cage? Do you sense your spirit breaking loose from bondages old and new? The old-timers had a phrase for these moments. They called it "waiting on God." You are living between "the already" and "the not yet." It's already promised, but it's not yet delivered. All you can do is wait on God—and that is the best thing to do when you are living in the land of potential, in the in-between zone. (*The God Catchers*, p. 95)

PRAYER

Father, I'm living in the land of potential as a refugee in the in-between zone. You are my only hope as I stand between the already promised and the not yet delivered. I'm waiting on You, and I'll just keep waiting on You until You come.

Collected Emptiness

*The Amount of Your Emptiness Determines
the Amount of Your Filling*

It is said that nature abhors a vacuum. Perhaps a greater truth should be said with even more emphasis: "He who is Fullness abhors all vacuums pretending to be full." We need Him, and to say anything else is folly and pretense.

Yet we have a certain ability to make our way through life under a surface pretense of inner strength and a sham of do-it-yourself success. Perhaps the reason is that we are created in His image.

All it takes is the specter of failure, collapse, disaster, or a glimpse of the one-way door of death to cause our hollow house of cards to fall.

The most irritating deception presented to Deity is the religious pretense of human fullness rooted in gathered knowledge, gathered good deeds, and gathered social accomplishment. These have no value in His sight. He can't work with these things; they are too full of themselves to accommodate any of His fullness.

The cure is emptiness—not the "nirvana" emptiness of religious asceticism, but the specific, detailed emptiness of spiritual hunger, thirst, passion, and longing for the heart and face of God. When this earthly treasure is collected and offered to Him, He responds personally, intimately, unforgettably, with His fullness. It is true: the amount of our emptiness determines the volume of our filling.

Human Fullness Is the Greatest Obstacle to Supernatural Filling

Some of us are determined to "present our fullness for God to fill." Then we complain to anyone who will listen that this "intimacy with God stuff" is a hoax. God isn't interested in meeting you at your best—that is really when you are at your worst. He isn't interested in blessing your independence; He responds to your dependence. His strength is attracted to your weakness. He casts down the proud, but He runs to the pitiful.[1]

THE GOD CATCHERS, P. 100

SCRIPTURE READING:

2 Kings 4:1–7, in which God uses a destitute widow to reveal how the volume of our spiritual hunger determines how much of His fullness we can receive.

Many confirmed God Chasers in this generation and in generations past share the common conviction that the powerlessness of the church stems from its prayerlessness and its habit of leaning on the weak arm of the flesh rather than on God.

It is easier to conduct church business and church worship gatherings according to cut-and-dried patterns, using the more easily controlled natural gifts and abilities of people, rather than admitting our reliance upon the irritatingly supernatural gifts and abilities of God. The problem is that by thinking and acting as if we can do a thing without God, it isn't His.

Take the time to examine your life and the life of your church. How much of what you do each day, and how much of the typical church service, is duplicated effortlessly in business offices, civic organizations, and country clubs every day? How much can be attributed solely to the intervention, provision, or personal visitation of God?

We can make people feel better through comforting words, and we can sound wise by delivering the wisdom of men packaged as the wisdom of God. We can even educate people in the Word of God without ever introducing them to the reality of His presence. Yes, their lives will be improved through their proximity to the truth, but they deserve more.

If we presume to "do church" in God's name, the least we should do is to lean upon His strength, wisdom, love, grace, and mercy with all of our ability (or should we say "inability"?). I don't remember John saying, "As many as are led by the habits, patterns, and programs of men, behold, they are the sons of God." Isn't the Spirit supposed to be involved somewhere in that process?

If we think we can "do church" using our human fullness without relying on His personal participation and supernatural visitation, then it seems logical that anyone can "do church" without God and have the same "unsupernatural" results. Unfortunately it is more than logical; it seems to be a way of life in much of the modern church world. (Is it any wonder that we are often powerless to transform lives, heal the sick, deliver the oppressed, and provide godly leadership in our cities?)

Is it wrong to meet needs using your natural gifts, wisdom, or accumulated knowledge? Is a God Chaser a hyperspiritual person who overspiritualizes even the mundane things of life? (*You know the answer to each question is no.*) How should you, as a God Chaser, remain dependent upon God and offer Him emptiness throughout the typical day so His supernatural fullness can invade the mundane?

The desperate widow and mother who encountered Elisha turned to God's fullness for relief when her life and the lives of her sons were endangered by the loss of her husband and the emptiness of her food pantry. She didn't offer God full bowls, pans, or containers. She didn't even limit her offering to her personal capacity for emptiness. Elisha the prophet told her to "collect emptiness" from her neighbors, so she scoured the area for every pot and pan she could.[2]

The widow didn't understand the importance of her collected emptiness, and neither do we most of the time. "She didn't realize that her cumulative emptiness would literally determine the measure of her miraculous filling" (*The God Catchers*, p. 99).

God loves to pour out His fullness on man's emptiness, but this won't happen until we run out (or willingly lay down) our strength, resources, ideas, programs, agendas, personal charisma, and "holy hyperbole." James said we "have seen the end of the Lord; that the Lord is very pitiful, and of tender mercy."[3] God is "full of pity" or compassionate. (*The God Catchers*, p. 100)

It may hurt, but I have to ask you: Are you full of yourself or full of His presence? What has the fullness in your life produced? What are you full of? What do you offer to Him?

PRAYER

Lord, my hunger can't be satisfied by anything in human pantries or on this planet. I have an unearthly appetite for heavenly things, especially for You. I want You. I've had my fill of earthly treasures, and they left me feeling emptier and more desperate than ever. Forgive me for offering You my fullness, and please accept my empty longing for Your presence.

God Searches for Passionate Pot and Pan Collectors

We shouldn't be content merely to present our own emptiness to the Father; we need to collect the emptiness and pain of those around us— exactly as Jesus taught us to do through His own example. Didn't I read somewhere that "He always lives to make intercession for them"?⁴ What do you live for?

THE GOD CATCHERS, P. 101

SCRIPTURE READING:

Ezekiel 22:29–30, where God describes His search for someone willing to "make a wall, and stand in the gap . . . on behalf of the land"; and Philippians 2:21, where the apostle Paul describes his search for someone to faithfully care for the church of Christ rather than seek his own.

Whether in the church or in our individual lives, the preoccupation with self and self-comfort looms as one of the greatest stumbling blocks in the Christian life. According to the Scriptures, God searches for worshipers and for people who will lay down their lives to stand in the gap—God's intercessors and anointed pot and pan collectors. These people look beyond their own needs and wants to "collect emptiness" from everyone their lives touch. Why? They offer the collective emptiness to the God of More Than Enough in return for His fullness on behalf of others.

Are you a holy pot and pan collector or a personal need and want seeker? Do you spend most of your time before the One who laid

126

down His life for you by seeking His blessings or by laying down your own life before Him on behalf of others?

It appears that you can collect emptiness from your neighbors as [the widow] did. In my mind, that is exactly what we are doing through intercessory prayer for our neighbors, schools, public officials, the government, and other nations. (*The God Catchers,* pp. 100–101)

Intercessory prayer isn't exactly the most popular activity on the Christian scene. Could that be because it is usually done beyond the view of the public eye, and because intercessors are rarely recognized, praised, or honored for the service they render on their knees? I'm reminded that intercession is the occupation Jesus chose after He defeated the enemy, rose from the dead, and took His seat at the right hand of the Father. Could we do any better?

Does the idea of intercessory prayer seem to be an odd match with the picture of a passionate God Chaser in hot pursuit of God's presence? Why? Every God Chaser of any consequence has been a person of deep and consistent prayer. How are your "knee skills"? How would you rank prayer—especially selfless intercessory prayer—as a "pursuit vehicle" in the chase for His presence?

God Chasers have no need to work up passion for God or compassion for others. If you intercede for others while you pursue Him, you will find yourself following the example of Jesus and feeling compassion on behalf of those God leads into your life.[5]

God says, "Pour out whatever oil you have. Empty yourself so I can fill you with more of Myself." The volume of your emptiness determines the amount of your filling. He can't fill anything more than what you present to Him. (*The God Catchers,* p. 101)

While you are gathering up the emptiness in your life, will you not take the time to gather up a few vessels of emptiness from those

around you and others God leads into your path? If you can increase the volume of the emptiness, you offer Him . . .

PRAYER

Father, I thought my hunger and thirst for You were measureless until I began to see the hunger and thirst in those around me. I've gathered them together in my heart, and I lift up all of these empty vessels to You along with my desperate longing to pray, "Fill us with Your fullness, Lord."

The Hungry Get Desperate, the Satisfied Become Apathetic

God is looking for really hungry people. He hopes to find them in the church, but if necessary, He will bypass an entire temple filled with dainty casual nibblers just to find a few really hungry people on the street, in a bar, or on the wrong side of town. Really hungry people tend to be really desperate people.

THE GOD CATCHERS, P. 102

SCRIPTURE READING:

Luke 6:20–22, where Jesus speaks directly to His disciples about the blessings in store for those suffering from heart hunger and spiritual thirst in the desolate and dangerous land of man's religion.

I've heard it said that many Americans are starving in the land of plenty—not because of the scarcity of food, because we have plenty, but because of the choices of food. Unfortunately this statement applies to the church as well. As I stated in *The God Catchers:*

Our problem is our diet. We like to stuff ourselves on spiritual junk food and feast on dainty bless-me treats. That is the kind of spiritual "food" that has all the form and outward appearance of godliness, but is a standing denial of its power. When the real meat and bread of His presence is placed in front of us, we turn away from His table of intimacy to look for another "quick and easy" flesh-blessing snack at the shallow-food bar. The unpleasant truth is that God is under no obligation to feed casual nibblers at His Communion table.[6] (p. 101)

Do you regard hunger as your friend or your enemy? Hunger nearly always feels uncomfortable and even painful, but what role does it play in your physical and spiritual well-being?

People who aren't hungry can easily walk past a banquet table offering the finest and most expensive foods, delicacies, and refreshments available to man. Hungry people, on the other hand, may feel stomach pains at the mere sight of a picture portraying the potential of food!

Satisfied Christians can attend a meeting where God manifests His presence and works miracles only to return to their homes unmoved and unimpressed with the departure from the usual in that service. Hungry God Chasers grow restless at the mere mention of a possible visitation by God, and they spend many of their waking hours anticipating the moment He manifests His presence once again.

Do you find it easy to attend worship services and leave without sensing God's presence? Does the mere mention of His possible visitation trigger spiritual hunger pains in your heart? Are you a chronic and incurable God Chaser?

People who aren't really hungry, especially those who enter His presence fresh from the bless-me church smorgasbord, tend to sample a little here and snack a little there with extended pinkies in mock discernment. They appear to be looking for "just the right feeling" or "just the right song" to get in the mood for communion with God.

. . . In the natural, true hunger can turn an honest man into a dishonest man, and it can transform a nonviolent man into a violent maniac. True hunger will make you do things you never, ever think you would do (in the natural and in the spiritual realm). (p. 102)

Do you casually nibble and search for favorite portions of each worship service, or do you enter every gathering feeling the desperation and urgency of a hungry soul, wondering, *Maybe this is the day He will visit us again?*

PRAYER

Lord Jesus, my soul aches at the mere mention of Your name. My heart leaps with every rumor of Your coming, and each possibility You will manifest Your presence. I'm not satisfied with mere spiritual dainties. I'm ravenously hungry for You in Your fullness. I'm desperate to feast on the bread of Your presence and quench my thirst with the wine of Your Spirit.

Plant Your Emptiness in the Field of His Fullness

When you collect emptiness or create emptiness by sowing what you have into the promises of God, you are living between the "already promised" and the "not yet delivered." You are "banking" on the faithfulness and compassion of God, who always responds to human emptiness with divine fullness.

Collected hunger cries out for His filling, and our collective collected hunger will basically determine how much of Him we will receive.

THE GOD CATCHERS, PP. 104–5

SCRIPTURE READING:

2 Corinthians 9:10–11, in which we find rich counsel in the sowing of our "emptiness seed" from a passage generally applied to finances in the kingdom.

Most people who live in agricultural areas or have some history rooted in the ancient occupation of farming understand the term "seed corn." They know that survival demands that a farmer set aside a portion of his best corn as a deposit on next year's crop (especially in developing nations where it may be impossible to purchase seed from a store or agricultural supply store). I put it this way in *The God Catchers*:

There is another way to "collect human emptiness" so you can receive divine fullness. It is rooted in God's law of seedtime and harvest. When a farmer prepares to plant seed in the ground, he must take seed corn off the storage shelf to invest it in the field of faith. In other words, he creates emptiness on his shelf to create fullness in the field for harvest.

132

For a while, it looks as if there is only emptiness in both places . . . The temporary emptiness created when you sow "what you have in your house" by faith produces an incredible filling. It is the law of the harvest, of sowing and reaping, in open display. (p. 104)

What emptiness do you have in your house that you can sow in the field of faith? Is there an emptiness in your neighbor's house or life that you can sow as seed corn on his or her behalf? Gather all of the lack you can to sow into His abundance, and remember that the volume of your harvest depends on the volume of your collective collected emptiness and lack!

I'm convinced that an unprecedented harvest is coming to the kingdom of God, a harvest so prolific that the harvesters will even overtake the sowers![7] However, the church in its present condition is too small in its thinking and too rigid in its ways and expectations to contain or properly care for such rapid growth. The church must change to provide biblical training and nurture for so many new Christians.

God wants to break outside our centuries-old religious box. That means our hunger has to get bigger than the box. We literally must have an uncontainable hunger for Him if we ever hope to accommodate and entertain His presence.[8]

Have you felt stretched and challenged by the Holy Spirit to change since you began chasing God's presence? Has it birthed a new excitement for the harvest in your heart? Are you willing to pay the personal price for such radical change?

PRAYER

Lord, I don't know what tomorrow holds, but I know I can't stay where I am today. You are on the move and I have no choice; my hunger forces me to move with my Source of supply. Change me; expand my heart and my mind to accommodate new frontiers of faith and boldness so I can play my part in Your purposes. My direction is uncertain, but my Goal is rock solid. I will follow You, Lord. My heart's desire is to dwell in Your presence all the days of my life.

Sow Fervent Cries of Emptiness and Hunger and Reap Supernatural Fullness (Revival)

Collected emptiness is one of the keys to citywide and nationwide revival because our collected and collective hunger may even cause God to bend the rules of the universe. Ask Moses! Ask Hezekiah! He has frozen the movements of the cosmos at the sound of a worshipful prayer.[9] *He has made the dead to rise and struck down the mighty and proud in response to the fervent cry of emptiness and hunger.*[10]

THE GOD CATCHERS, P. 105

SCRIPTURE READING:

Exodus 3:7–10, where God ambushes Moses with destiny, and He says the cries and suffering of His people motivated their divine encounter.

When hunger leads you to His feet and your heart burns with the wonder of His love, you begin to share the very passions of God's heart. The same passionate love that led Jesus to lay down His life to save you and me will ignite new passion and vision in your heart for revival in your generation and the generations to come.

All of the great revivals of the past were launched when the dry tender of hungry human souls came into contact with the spark of God's passionate love for the human race. In other words, God uses human torches—God Chasers filled to the point of spontaneous combustion—to light the fires of revival in cities, nations, and entire generations!

Are you filled with His passion and compassion to the point of spontaneous combustion? Are you prepared to become a torch in God's hand, a God Catcher caught in His embrace?

It is possible to start a fire with a single spark carried in one human heart, but it is much better to start a firestorm using the *collected* heat and energy of many sparks bound together in a single torch of fierce heat. Change your thinking if necessary to include the collected hunger, thirst, and emptiness of those you encounter each day.

Offer that collective collected emptiness to the God of More Than Enough in faith, and expect a harvest of His fullness great enough to fill every empty space your gift represents. Believe Him for a visitation and habitation of God's glory that will overwhelm every device, scheme, work, and accomplishment of the enemy in the process.

Do you concentrate solely on offering God your hunger and emptiness, or are you willing to reach out and collect the emptiness of others as well? It can be costly, but are you willing to make the investment in tomorrow's harvest?

Why should we gather the emptiness of other people and offer it to God? Isn't that greedy? No, the only way to follow in Jesus' footsteps is to give up our lives in His name and lay down our lives for others. We are not after a modest shaking; we want a full-blown, all-out earthquake of His glory that is too large to be registered on the Richter scale or any other scale for that matter. The reason is clear:

Revival is not a natural process of time; revival occurs only when eternity visits time. Revival requires supernatural intervention and the suspension of natural processes because you really only have revival when "something that is dead comes back to life." (*The God Catchers,* p. 106)

Are you prepared to cry out for a resurrection of the dead? Openly display your hunger and desperation for eternity's visit to time. Cry

out for Him to manifest His glory in this generation, and revival will simply be a by-product of His nearness to our needs.

True wide-scale revival requires a supernatural encounter with the manifested presence of God. This happens when we create and collect emptiness by diverting our hunger from man to Him. Remember, "blessed are those who hunger and thirst for righteousness, for they shall be filled."[11]

PRAYER

Lord, I'm diverting all of my hunger away from man to focus it on You. I'm hungry. I'm thirsty. I know I'm blessed, but I'm not content to stop there. There are too many hungry and desperate people around me who don't know the wonder of Your presence. I'm after nothing less than an explosive encounter with You of such magnitude that it shakes everything that can be shaken.

Let Hunger Lift You Higher and Closer to Him

I confess to you that if there is a secret that I could leave with you in this book, it is this: your hunger will take you to places in God that nothing else can. Hunger for Him can take you higher and move His presence closer to you than you ever dreamed. By God's design, He is moved and attracted by the hunger of the human heart.

THE GOD CATCHERS, P. 108

SCRIPTURE READING:

Isaiah 55:6–13, where the prophet says, "Seek the Lord while He may be found, call upon Him while He is near."

We are too easily satisfied with stories of someone else's encounter with Him . . . If you are tired of merely hearing about the God encounters other people had, then start collecting and creating emptiness. The same hunger that drove them into His presence will transport you into His presence too. Is your stomach growling yet? Can you feel the hunger pangs starting to grow in strength and frequency?[12]

Christians hide their hunger just as people with leprosy hide their disfigured limbs. We also disguise our passion with pasted-on faces and rigid limbs in fear that our peers will uncover our "dirty secret" and drown us in their self-righteous disapproval.

What if the very things we consider demeaning to the Christian faith are actually the fuel of God's fire in our hearts? Release the hunger you are hiding behind your rags of outward righteousness. Remove every false disguise, peel away every layer of fake piety, and openly display your passionate desperation for His presence. Focus your thoughts on Him and His holiness; let holy hunger pangs grip your soul and transport you where you've never been before. Seek the Lord while He may be found. Call upon Him while He is near!

The level of passion is increasing. Are you feeling more uncomfortable or more at home as the spiritual temperature rises? Why?

Unlike man, God is more interested in your tears of repentance and cries of desperation than in the sharpness of your creases and the size of your offerings. He delights in mascara-stained faces and elaborate hairdos draped across tear-stained carpets. He rejoices over humbled kings of commerce and brokenhearted barons of business and enterprise. It is only the proud that He ignores.

What will you offer Him? Proud religious accomplishments garnished with proper public piety, or tearful cries of repentance and hunger soaked in the fiery sauce of desperation? Which would He accept, and which would He reject?

Our churches have been guilty of false representation and false advertising long enough. We've claimed to be the bride of Christ while conducting our business and going our own way as if we were separated from Him. It is time to return the *supernatural* part of God's nature to God's house. If we dare to claim, "God is here!" then we better be prepared to do what it takes to back up our claim. In *The God Catchers,* I said,

> For too long the church has trumpeted to the nations, "He's here! He's here!" when there wasn't enough of Him there to make the church discernibly different from the world. Our claims were true in the sense that the omnipresent God was present in our churches, but that is no claim to fame. His omnipresence is everywhere, even in bars and nightclubs. It's His manifest presence that we must become hungry for, those undeniable moments when you know . . . *He's here!* (p. 109)

Are you hungry for more of Him than you have ever experienced? Will you pay the price to stay in His presence? The world is waiting

and hoping that we really will produce evidence of the Real Thing. Call upon His name and offer Him your uninhibited, unshackled hunger for His presence.

PRAYER

Father, I'm removing every self-generated and self-maintained religious disguise and pretense from my life. I refuse to maintain a lie any longer. I am so hungry for You that I will even risk rejection from others so I can draw close to You.

The Best God Chasers
Are Skilled Emptiness Collectors

God is shopping for the place of the next outbreak, *a place where He can pour out His presence in such volume and power that it will impact people far beyond the four walls of our church buildings . . .*

God has enough glory to flood the earth to overflowing. The problem isn't whether or not God is enough. The only things that determine how much oil of His presence flows among us is how empty we are and how much unity we can collect.

THE GOD CATCHERS, P. 111

SCRIPTURE READING:

Numbers 14:20–21, where God answers the intercessory plea of Moses to forgive the Israelites, and then declares the whole earth will be covered with His glory.

If you had ten million dollars to give away, would you be careless when deciding where to place that money? I hope not just any recipient would do because the only predictable aspect of undisciplined human nature is its ability to squander, misuse, and abuse resources without forethought or consideration of consequences.

God is very particular about where He places His treasure, and its worth is beyond earthly measure. In fact, He prefers to deliver it personally to two or more of us at a time, and preferably while we are in the posture of worship, the ultimate position of humility and selflessness.

How would you characterize the spiritual posture you maintain most of the time? Do you stand proud before Him to assert your biblical rights? Are you seated (and half asleep) most of the time, or does He find you most often approaching and chasing Him from the position of humility, passionate adoration, and continuous need?

When God's manifested presence comes down to us in response to our worship, He doesn't come to you on one side or to me on the other side of the mercy seat. He comes right in the middle of us. Didn't Jesus say, "Where two or three are gathered together in My name, I am there in the midst of them"?[13] He always comes in the middle, and the size of that middle space, the collected and collective sum total of our corporate emptiness, determines how much of Him comes. Wherever you gather with one or more fellow worshipers in His name, He will come in the middle of your collective emptiness. (*The God Catchers,* p. 110)

This concept of offering God emptiness may seem strange, but it is thoroughly biblical. It amounts to leveling or confessing the truth to God each time we meet. The truth is that no matter how high we climb in our walk of faith, we still need His infinite grace and mercy simply to draw our next breath.

Each moment of life is a gift from His hand that we must never take lightly. Jesus gave us Scripture for offering the Father emptiness when He told His disciples in blunt, no-exception-to-the-rule terms, "If anyone desires to come after Me, let him deny himself, and take up his cross daily, and follow Me."[14] That means you must "deny utterly, disown and abstain from, contradict, refuse, and reject" yourself and take up your cross every day.[15] That sounds like a good way to offer Him your emptiness each day.

How do you collect emptiness in your life? How do you collect collective emptiness in your family, in the local church, and in your city or region?

Can I say again that the real harbinger of revival is not a good preacher or a good singer? It is the amount of our collected hunger. I repeat, God is inexorably drawn to the empty capacity of our growling spiritual stomachs when we gather in one mind and one accord with an unappeasable appetite for Him. (*The God Catchers*, p. 112, italics mine)

PRAYER

God, I am desperately hungry for You. I don't lift up my fullness because I have none. All I have to offer You is my collected emptiness, a holy vacuum that can be filled only by Your presence. I need You! My vessel is empty and my future is in jeopardy.

I openly display my desperation and utter dependence upon You. I humble myself and create emptiness so that You might create fullness. I anticipate the joy of a harvest of Your presence in me. Come fill me, Holy Spirit. (*The God Catchers*, p. 112)

How to Carry Hot Coffee

Retaining the Fresh Deposit of God

How many times have you heard someone confidently remark about a difficult goal such as a sports championship or the acquisition of something valuable, "It is one thing to get it, but it is another thing to keep it"?

I've heard the same remark offered in countless discussions about revival. The believers who operate in the unlisted gift of pessimism publicly wonder why we even bother with revival if it is going to go away, leaving us more depressed than when we began.

The remark about the difficulty of keeping revival is true; the comment about not bothering with revival is not. I can't speak for everyone, but I would rather fall in love once than never fall in love at all. Besides, it is possible to keep the fresh deposit of God.

It seems I read somewhere that as we behold Him, we are transformed into His image "from glory to glory."[1] Our problem is spiritual coordination: we must learn how to carry God's hot coffee with one hand while carrying our cross with the other.

Do You Know How to Carry Heaven's Hot Coffee?

How do you carry the fresh encounter of God in your inward vessel? How does a church body guard the divine deposit from one worship experience to the next? How do you "take this home" in real life?

Walk carefully and be aware of His every movement in your heart. Whether you are driving your car, leading worship, preaching a sermon, or bathing your baby, if you feel Him softly tap your shoulder, then "fold up the letter" and turn to look into His face. When He invades your empty space of hunger, turn to meet Him in your spirit. Answer His gentle summons as the young man named Samuel did; he tentatively called out into the darkness of his empty room, "Speak, for Your servant hears."

THE GOD CATCHERS, PP. 115–16

SCRIPTURE READING:

1 Samuel 3:1–10, in which we see Samuel walk through the process of recognizing God's voice as distinct from the voice of Eli, his spiritual teacher and mentor.

We all go through various rites of passage in our lives—the first feeble attempts to roll over, to walk, to talk, to dress ourselves; the first time we notice the opposite sex; the first time we drive a car. Almost without exception, our first attempts at these things are tentative and awkward. Through the natural process of trial and error, we ultimately move past the awkward stage, and such things become second nature to us in time. God wants each of us to go through Samuel's rite of passage as well, where we learn to recognize and heed His voice for ourselves.

The first time He tends to come suddenly. After that, you may encounter Him unexpectedly as you earnestly chase Him and seek His face. Prepare a place of hunger, desire, worship, and praise for Him, and invite Him to turn aside and dwell with you. "What do You want, Lord? How can we bless and host You tonight, Lord?" (*The God Catchers,* p. 116)

Has the Lord ever invaded your empty space of hunger? What did you do when it happened the first time? Did you handle things differently the next time?

The next phase takes us beyond the realm of communication and into the task of transportation and distribution. Jesus died on the cross to accomplish more than to save our souls; He wanted to duplicate Himself through us. None of us can begin to measure up to Him individually, but we can do the works of Christ together as one body (that is what the Great Commission is all about).

When God visits us and deposits His manifested glory among us, He expects us to carefully guard and carry His divine deposit in two directions: we carry it back into our worship gatherings so our carrying capacity can be increased even more, and we carry the light of His presence into the darkness to make disciples of the lost.

Are you willing to walk carefully to carry and preserve His divine deposit when you go home, return to the workplace, shop at the store, or participate in nonchurch activities during the week? Do you think this is really necessary, or should "spiritual stuff" be reserved for the few hours you actually spend in a church building each week? (*This is what I call "God-in-a-Box Religion."*)

PRAYER

Father, I'm determined to walk carefully while carrying the hot deposit You have poured into my life. Your presence is too precious to be wasted or lost through careless handling. Holy Spirit, help me hear Your still small voice and sense Your gentle tap on my shoulder. Give me ears to hear and eyes to see what You have for me. Then teach me how to carry heaven's "hot coffee," the holy deposit of God's manifest presence, from glory to glory and into the wounded world of the lost in Jesus' name.

If You Can Carry More, You Will Receive More

If you can return to your worship gathering or private devotions without spilling anything God deposited in your heart, then you won't have to start over. You can go on from this deposit of glory to the next level in Him, moving from "glory to glory." [2] The goal is to increase your capacity to carry His presence and His light into the realm of darkness.

THE GOD CATCHERS, P. 117, EMPHASIS MINE

SCRIPTURE READING:

Matthew 25:14–29, where Jesus links faithfulness with increased capacity in the parable of the talents (or divine deposit).

Even casual readers of the New Testament passages should notice two outstanding things about God and the church. First, it is clear that the Father expects every member of His family to be a *working member.* He never envisioned a house full of couch potatoes planted in front of the Holy Spirit television waiting for Daddy to come home with the groceries.

Second, it is also clear that we are to imitate the actions of Jesus Christ by caring for others more than for ourselves.[3] That takes us right back to the final words of Jesus:

Go therefore and make disciples of all the nations, baptizing them in the name of the Father and of the Son and of the Holy Spirit, teaching them to observe all things that I have commanded you; and lo, I am with you always, even to the end of the age.[4]

Many of us resent it, but God expects us to take on more carrying capacity as we grow up in Him. We've done everything we can to remove one specific dirty four-letter word from our church vocabulary (w-o-r-k), but God keeps bringing it up again. The more we know, the more we should go. The more we can do, the more we should do. Perhaps our failure to be faithful in the most basic things explains His unwillingness to entrust us with His divine deposit of glory.

How would you classify yourself—as a working member of God's household, or as a lounging member waiting for more groceries? Is your local church casually consuming God's groceries to satisfy its own appetite, or is it seeking a divine deposit to make new disciples by transporting the bread of His presence to hungry hearts in the world?

Are you really serious about an ongoing habitation of the glory of God? Do you seriously believe you can literally change the environment of your home, your job site, and community? If His presence is involved, then I believe it too. Do you honestly expect to draw the lost and hungry in your family and community to Jesus Christ? It won't happen if you try to do it by cramming doctrine down their throats. On the other hand, if you can make them so hungry for His presence that nothing else matters, then I will believe it too. (*The God Catchers*, p. 116)

Once I encountered the reality of God's manifest presence in my life, I had to redefine and restructure my ideas about ministry. From that point on, I was more interested in *imparting hunger for His presence* than in delivering information about His nature. We do need information about God's nature, but we need impartation of hunger for His presence even more. Even the demons of hell possess and believe basic information about God,[5] but they will *never* possess a hunger for His presence. Such an encounter with unveiled Deity is the substance of hell's most persistent nightmares.

The more you encounter His presence, the more of Him you want. God hunger is catching because God ordained it that way. I've visited countless church congregations that define their corporate mission with the phrase

"That we may know Him and make Him known." This is a perfect description of what it means to be a God Chaser.

How do you define your mission from God? Is it "to receive blessings from Him and ask for more," or "to know Him and make Him known"? How would you define the mission of Jesus' earthly ministry? Did He primarily impart information about the Father or hunger for relationship with the Father?

Love your friends, hug your kids, go out to eat, laugh and talk, but *remember that God has deposited something supernatural in you.* Walk carefully so you won't "spill" any. (*The God Catchers,* p. 117, italics mine)

PRAYER

Father, I am thankful for everything I've learned about Your nature and about Your past dealings with humanity, but I want more. I want to know You. I want to see Your face and experience Your glory. Thank You for every blessing You have showered upon my life and upon the church, but please show me Your face. Fill me with more and more of Your presence, and anoint me to transport more and more of Your light to those in darkness.

We Need More Box-Breaker Marys

Learn to carry His presence so you can become a contagious carrier. King David discovered that God's glory (represented by the ancient ark of the covenant) was meant to be carried on the shoulders of men, not on man-made platforms or devices . . .

We still try to carry His glory on the "ox carts" of our man-made, man-driven programs or evangelistic formulas. We prefer them because they are easier, they are more predictable, and they are softer on the flesh that dominates many of our services.

THE GOD CATCHERS, P. 117

SCRIPTURE READING:

Romans 12:1–2, where Paul describes the minimum "sacrifice" all New Testament believers are required to give to God.

In 1931, U.S. researchers coined a name for people who are contagious carriers of diseases. It happened after they traced an outbreak of typhoid to an Irish cook named Mary Mallon, who was working in the United States. Even to this day most people remember Typhoid Mary as the woman who carried a disease without being consumed by it.

Another Mary has been remembered for two thousand years because she carried a costly alabaster box of perfume into another person's house just to break it and anoint Jesus with its costly fragrance as an act of worship. Her act of worship forever marked Box-Breaker Mary as a carrier of a divine disease, an affliction marked by incurable and contagious hunger for God's presence.[6]

What spiritual "disease" are you spreading wherever you go? Are you a contagious carrier of holy hunger, groundless gossip, or pathetic apathy? Are you willing to pay the price to be a Box-Breaker Mary or a Damascus Road Paul?

Carrying God's presence from one place to another isn't easy, but it is mandatory nonetheless. This statement may sound radical, but it is accurate. I read somewhere that "it is the God who commanded light to shine out of darkness, who has shone in our hearts to give the light of the knowledge of the glory of God in the face of Jesus Christ. But we have this treasure in earthen vessels, that the excellence of the power may be of God and not of us."[7]

God deposits the knowledge of His glory in human vessels, and He wants us to walk in unity so the light of His presence can be pooled, concentrated, amplified, and expanded to flood the earth with His glory.[8] That means we must learn how to carry His divine deposit into our worship gatherings and back out into the world to minister to those in need. As noted in *The God Catchers,* "The truth is that the presence of God comes on the shoulders of men and women, and it always has. A program will never usher the presence of God into a church" (pp. 117–18).

No matter how we look at it, we must increase our skills and enlarge our capacity to carry God's glory when He makes the divine deposit.

How hungry are you for His presence? Will you risk rejection and brave ejection to carry your alabaster box for Him, no matter what the cost?

PRAYER

Lord, I'll be a Box Breaker for You. Make a divine deposit in my life, and I'll offer my earthen vessel back to You. I'm so desperate for Your presence that I offer my life as an alabaster box to be broken before You to fill my world with the fragrance of Your presence. My life is not my own, for I've been bought with a price.

Prepare a Meal
and the Hungry Will Come

I have a recurring dream that some Sunday morning, the hunger of God's people will reach such white-hot levels that it will create the habitation of the Holy Spirit. That morning, all the restaurant managers in the city will wonder, Where is the Sunday morning crowd? All this food is going to waste.

Hour by hour goes by and not one Baptist, Methodist, Presbyterian, Brethren, Church of Christ, or Pentecostal shows up at the food bar. Why? The glory of God has broken over the city, and visitation has become habitation. Everyone is so busy dining at the table of His presence that no one even thinks about pulling up at a natural dinner table.

THE GOD CATCHERS, P. 119

SCRIPTURE READING:

Revelation 19:7–9, where John sees the great marriage supper of the Lamb, which perfectly pictures the joy and feasting we enjoy in this life when God's people lay aside every tool of division to feast on the bread of His presence.

People may easily dismiss God Chasers as mere thrill seekers as long as they have never experienced the manifestation of God's presence. Once a critic personally experiences the celestial thrill of divine visitation he will understand the heart of God addiction. (A status change will be in order because the job title of "critic" will no longer apply.)

There is something about the bread of His presence that reduces everything else on man's religious menu to the status of yesterday's second-rate leftovers.

When God shows up in His concentrated presence, everything we've read about in His Word suddenly becomes real in a new way.

Pastors discover they no longer have to labor in the Word to encourage the sheep to feed on God's Word. Suddenly God's people discover a new appetite for everything related to God and His purposes. They can't consume enough of the Bible; they find themselves sharing the gospel with anything and everything that moves. They feel compelled to unload, give out, pour out, and share the divine abundance that exudes from every pore of their beings. That is simply to be expected when God's fullness visits man's emptiness.

Are you still evaluating the God Chaser syndrome as if it were an illness to be cured, or have you caught the disease that is nearly as exciting as its Cure? Have you ever caught Him? If so, are you cured, or are you even more determined to pursue Him while passing on your divine disease to others?

The only way God's presence will break out over an entire city and region is if His people learn how to entertain His presence in their undying hunger for Him and carry it with them. This kind of hunger burns so brightly that it gives no place to "respect of persons" or personal agendas. Labels and religious jargon fall away and lose their power in its heat. The only thing hunger will recognize is the Source of its satisfaction. (*The God Catchers,* p. 119)

Throughout human history, wise men and women have understood that the best way to draw a crowd (whether it is a crowd of people or a herd of beasts) is to throw a feast. Movie theater managers make sure the smell of buttered popcorn wafts through their theaters while large full-color pictures of mouth-watering refreshments form a feast for the eyes. Television advertisers know how to tweak every wish, desire, and lust in human nature. And nearly every open house of any kind in American culture includes a spread of assorted dainties, drinks, and delectable desserts to attract a crowd.

None of these things can begin to compare with the attraction of divine visitation in human habitations. The appearance of the Real Thing ignites unbearable human hunger for supernatural satisfaction.

What kind of hunger do you ignite in the hearts of the people around you? Does the perfume of His presence linger when you enter a room of hungry souls? What kind of "table" have the churches of the city set for the hungry souls who live there? Are you offering them stale crumbs of past visitations or the fresh bread of His presence?[9]

What would happen if the glory of God broke over your entire city or region? Think of the far-reaching effects it would have on the people who live there.

Are you willing to stand in the gap until God breaks out over your city? . . . Some people automatically assume that "this God Chaser stuff" is all about the selfish pursuit of just another "religious buzz." No, it is all about God and His purposes, not about us. (*The God Catchers,* p. 119)

PRAYER

Lord, make me a tool of eternal hunger in Your hand. Permeate me with Your presence to the point that Your fragrance lingers and fills every room I enter. May an unavoidable hunger of the heart seize everyone I meet, whether saved or unsaved. May all hearts turn to You when I pass through a room.

Guard the Divine Deposit— Keep Your Eyes on Him

Anytime God visits you with a miracle, an outpouring of His Spirit, or the beginnings of true revival, the enemy will come and attempt to steal the promise and destroy the deposit the Lord gave you.

THE GOD CATCHERS, P. 121

SCRIPTURE READING:

John 10:9–14, where Jesus says He is the Door to God's kingdom and the abundant life, and immediately warns us that the thief comes only to steal, kill, and destroy.

Peter the disciple understood the dangerous period that immediately follows the glorious moments of miracles, outpourings, revelation, and glory. He was minding his own business after a long hike to a northern town just below Mount Hermon when the lightbulb of revelation suddenly came on.

After the disciples told Jesus what everyone else was saying about His identity, He asked who they believed He was, and Peter blurted out what all of creation had been waiting to hear: "You are the Christ, the Son of the living God."[10]

Have you experienced a mountaintop event after a momentous God encounter, ministry success, or successful faith walk far beyond your own ability? Did you sense the need to be on watch for an attack or temptation just around the corner? Were you right?

It wasn't long before disaster struck Peter's life. When Jesus began to explain that He was destined to die on the cross, Peter apparently felt that new authority as an anointed "seer" qualified him to judge and rebuke the Son of God for negative thinking.

Merely seven verses after Peter received praise from Jesus for his prophetic insight, he heard Jesus say things no man (or church body) wants to hear: "Get behind Me, Satan! You are an offense to Me, for you are not mindful of the things of God, but the things of men."[11]

How many times have you caught yourself (or been caught by some-one else) thinking more about what men might think than about what God might think? Is this a warning to churches as well?

Most of the time, the thief called Satan is too smart to tempt God's people with "big" sins. His best saint fishing success comes with lures dressed up in church habits and traditions. As long as the end result displeases God, Satan has no problem using some of the greatest blessings of God to attract godly people to his hook.

Unfortunately God's visitation rarely turns into habitation because of our human tendency to immediately turn our focus away from His face to concentrate on the "good feelings" His presence creates in our bodies and souls. These side benefits are wonderful, but we must keep our central focus on God, not on the pleasant side effects of His presence. (*The God Catchers*, p. 120)

Have you ever asked God to meet a need in a time of crisis and then become so preoccupied with His miracle blessing that you neglected to thank Him for it or return to your position of worship? Have you spent more time seeking revival than seeking the Reviver?

Success without humility sets the stage for failure, just as spiritual satisfaction without fresh hunger for God's presence may become the breeding ground for spiritual apathy. The moment we turn our attention from His face to measure and compare what we received against what others received, we begin to lay a foundation for strife and division. It is more important than ever after a visitation of God for us to leave our worship services hungrier than when we came.

> I know of many cities where a measure of His glory visited and major revival broke out. Thousands of people received Jesus Christ as Lord and Savior in these cities. Many of these visitations began during an interchurch search for God's presence, with several congregations and pastors working closely together in one mind and one accord. Later, just as the visitation began to look more and more like habitation, interchurch differences turned to strife and grieved the Holy Spirit. (*The God Catchers,* pp. 120–21)

Where do you keep your focus? Are you locked into His gaze, His presence, and His beauty, or do you take breaks to measure and compare yourself against other God Chasers? Are you prepared to keep your hand to the plow and not look back or to the side? As long as you keep your eyes on Him, you won't have to worry about what others are doing. It is all in His hands.

PRAYER

Lord, I want You. Grant me the wisdom to keep my focus on You and Your kingdom rather than on the opinions and approval of mankind. I will keep my eyes upon You, not upon Your many blessings. I want more than a temporary passing visitation; I long for an abiding habitation of Your presence. I take David's dream as my own: "One thing I have desired of the Lord, that will I seek: That I may dwell in the house of the Lord all the days of my life, to behold the beauty of the Lord."[12]

Do You Know How to Catch God in His Promises?

Has your divine promise from God dropped dead in the field of dreams? Is your hope for a miracle lingering between a comatose state and a grave of adverse circumstances? Have you watched the children God gave you slip away into sin, rebellion, or bad company while your heart broke for the hundredth time?

It is time to lay the broken, fallen, and dying things in your life on the bed of worship in the room of praise that you prepared for Him. It isn't over until God says it is over.

THE GOD CATCHERS, P. 123

SCRIPTURE READING:

2 Kings 4:8–37, where we discover how a non-Jewish woman managed to catch God in His promises even before the death and resurrection of Christ.

Why would Jesus forewarn us about the nature and strategy of the thief who opposes us unless it was possible to anticipate and overcome his assault? Every Christian should already know the basic fundamentals of putting on the armor of God,[13] and of the power given to us through the shed blood and the name of Jesus Christ.[14] Yet even good and godly people will experience attacks of the enemy, and virtually all of us will know the reality of the death of a vision or the challenge of a promise delayed or seemingly denied.

A woman in Elisha the prophet's day discovered this unpleasant pattern, but her careful preparation met the enemy's attack head-on. The key is that she made room for God's presence in advance. Her example offers clues for your own preparations for the habitation of God and the enemy's attempt to kill or steal His divine deposit . . .

This woman had enough discernment to perceive the anointed mission and calling of Elisha. She had enough wisdom to want more of a holy visitation and enough determination to follow through on her plan to entertain the prophetic presence. *She knew how to "catch" God in His promises.* (*The God Catchers,* pp. 121–22, italics mine)

Have you remodeled your life and prepared a room for God's presence? Have you prepared a habitation for divinity in your humanity through your brokenness, hunger, passionate worship, and adoration for Him?

If you build Him a place of praise fitted with a bed of worship, you may discover that when "a day of trial and tribulation comes, that room you prepared for holy visitation will become a room of omnipotent intervention."[15] Learn to fall to your knees and seek His face instead of standing to your feet and clenching your fist to rage at the circumstances.

Do you have a place of visitation where you can rest your dead or dying visions and hopes? Begin to prepare for His habitation now, even before He shows up. You have to create the empty space and furnish it with your hunger, your worship, and your praise. (*The God Catchers,* p. 124)

PRAYER

Father, I have the promise of Your Word: "Blessed are the poor in spirit . . . Blessed are those who hunger and thirst for righteousness, for they shall be filled."[16] You visited once, so I know You will come back again. The next time You show up, I'm going to be ready for You. I'm thankful for what You've done, Lord, but I want to see what You can do. (*The God Catchers,* p. 124)

Are You Prepared for God to Say Yes?

Are you ready for His visitation, Pastor? Have you prepared for the coming of the One you've asked for, sir? Have you prepared for His presence, Mom? God visited you before, and He will come again—make everything ready for the King of glory. The next time He visits, will He discover the empty space of hunger and desire you have made for Him alone?

THE GOD CATCHERS, P. 124

SCRIPTURE READING:

1 Peter 2:11-12, where the seasoned apostle urges believers whose lives have been changed by God to live honestly among the unsaved so they will give glory to God in the "day of visitation."

If revivals seem to come and go on the human landscape while the Reviver remains the same yesterday, today, and forever, what is missing from the equation? The answer must at least include the changing levels of our hunger for His manifest presence. In other cases, a lack of knowledge about His Word played a part. In other times, perhaps the sins of key leaders brought disrepute on the kingdom and annulled the work of the Spirit. However, it seems that in every case God manages to have a hungry remnant pass through the fires of adversity to rekindle the coals of worship and set the stage for His return.

I've revisited many historic places where God visited. Satan always tries to steal the divine deposit. In many of those places, a hungry remnant are carefully preparing a place with no agenda but their raw hunger and desperation for God. They want His fresh deposit, they are walking carefully, and they believe by faith that He will pass their way again. They are right; He will. (*The God Catchers,* p. 124)

Are you preparing a place for Him? Do you have an agenda, or are you operating out of sheer hunger and desperation for His presence? Are you willing to pay the price for a fresh deposit of God's presence?

One of the things I've learned as a God Chaser is the importance of relinquishment in our daily discipline. Many times the Reviver cannot give us the desire of our hearts because our hands, lives, and ministries are filled with the desires of our flesh.

I'm not limiting the desires of the flesh to the most blatant sins of misplaced or uncontrolled sexual appetite, chemical and drug addiction, or amoral ethics and conduct. Some of the greatest offenders before God are the sins of the flesh dressed in the trappings of church.

What would we have to relinquish or give up to carry or entertain His presence? The answer is anything that turns our focus away from Him and back toward us. Some of the chief offenders that turn up in conversations with pastors around the world include religious traditions, rigid congregational or denominational worship patterns, personal habits and preferences, and fixed personal or organizational agendas. (*The God Catchers,* p. 125)

God hasn't changed. Whether we are saved or unsaved, He requires us to empty ourselves to be filled with His presence. He refuses to bunk up with our favorite secret sins, our selfishness, or even the church doctrines we idolize in place of the Head of the church. As I said in *The God Catchers,* "Some of us need a miracle of God to release our grip on our families and our brethren. So be it" (p. 126). His fullness is worth the effort it takes to empty our hands and hearts of second-best things any day.

Are you prepared to say no to yourself so He can say yes to your hungry cry? Are you prepared to release your things so you can receive Him? Are you desperate enough to entertain Him and make a habitation for His presence?

PRAYER

Father, I am pitiful; I'm running out of words, and I don't know how to do what You have called me to do.

Holy Spirit, I know there is a place of Your presence in which our lives are changed. Once we encounter You there, we will never be the same.

We call for holy habitation. We join our passionate cries with the cry of Moses: Please show us Your face!

We are passionate for one thing—You. Set our hearts on fire with hunger; make us miserably desperate for more of You. Set Your hot coal of hunger and holiness on our tongues and in our hearts. We long for You.

Let Your fire burn in our churches; let the fire blaze in our homes. It's not a man that we want; we want You, Lord. Show us Your face, God. (*The God Catchers*, pp. 127–28)

The Secret of the Stairs

The Bride's Access to the Heart of God

Humanity may view the church as an institution with social and political characteristics, but God has called her His bride from the beginning. We would never apply the language of intimacy to our relationship with an institution. Perhaps that helps explain the condition of a church that at times seems stranded far from the place of intimacy with God described in the Bible.

A season of change has come. Fresh currents of rising passion and longing are tugging at the heart of the church, gently urging her back to her first love. As her members answer the call of love, those who yield to their longing for His presence are rediscovering the ancient path of access to the very heart of God.

The bride has resumed her preparations for union with her Beloved, and renewed passion is leading her once again to the secret places of the stairs.

Where Are the People of the Inner Chamber?

When someone shows you his hidden key, he has given you family privileges.
God has shown us His hidden key—the key to His heart and the secret place of access to divine intimacy. In the Authorized Version, Solomon called it "the secret places of the stairs."

THE GOD CATCHERS, P. 131

SCRIPTURE READING:

Song 2:14, where Solomon unveils the secret places of the stairs reserved solely for his adoring beloved and paints a prophetic portrait of the privileged access the Messiah has reserved only for His bride, the worshiping church.

In the rare times when I sit down and watch an evening news program on television, I'm fascinated when I see a crowd of TV reporters, journalists, photographers, and gawkers pressing against a police line outside the home of a celebrity or political figure.

The TV reporters pose for the cameras in strategic locations with the front door of the house in view while they proudly postulate and elaborate on the latest rumors about those who live inside. Photographers snap photographs of the swirling crowd and the unopened doors while journalists shout questions at the police and interview gawkers for man-on-the-street impressions. No one has access to the facts or the people they concern because no one has privileged access to the house or its occupants.

Everything goes into high gear the moment a family member arrives (with a police escort if she has had well-informed advice). The crowd reluctantly parts so the one person with privileged access can make her way to the door and enter the privacy of the house—leaving behind scores of frustrated fact and fiction gatherers doomed to permanent separation from the object of their interest inside the house.

Sometimes I wonder whether we've built much of what we call church around secondhand musings, opinions, and educated guesses about the Object of our interest—provided by people who may never have entered the inner chambers of God's habitation.

It should be obvious that God doesn't mind if we enter His "house" and prepare refreshments for Him in anticipation of His manifest presence there. Especially since He's given us the key!

Unfortunately centuries of bad human decisions and our attraction to the stuff of religion muddied the waters of our privileged grace relationship with divinity. We have used man-centered, religion-based traditions and methods to rebuild the walls that divide God and man—after Jesus shed His precious blood to break them down. (*The God Catchers,* p. 131)

Do you feel as if you've spent most of your life outside the habitation of God, even though you have attended your share of church services? How can you pass through the swirling crowds and confusion outside to enter the place of His presence? Is there a secret passage or entrance?

Part of the problem is our preoccupation with the opinions and whims of men. As I noted in *The God Catchers,* "We plan our services, craft our sermons, and sing our songs to move men, but where is the church that knows how to move the heart of God?" (p. 133). The Scriptures warn that the fear of man is a trap or a snare;[1] but most of us are afraid or unwilling to admit that we have a man-fear problem. The time has come for honesty and boldness. God has given us a key; now He is waiting for someone bold enough to use it.

Do you know how to move the heart of God? Do you have a man-fear problem to give to Him? You have the key. Now what will you do with it?

Where are the people who know Him so intimately that their worship and adoration can almost "change" His mind? Where are the people of the inner chamber, the intimate companions of God who are so in tune with His heart that others seek them out for advice on how to approach the King? God wants to raise up a generation of God-pleasers, not the run-of-the-mill religious man-pleasers. Our destiny is founded upon His wisdom and purposes, not the ever-changing whims and wishes of men. That means the church desperately needs people who possess the secret of the stairs Solomon alluded to in his Song of Songs. (*The God Catchers,* p. 134)

Are you encouraged and inspired to become a person of the inner chamber? Will you pay the price to possess the secret of the stairs and become an intimate companion of God?

PRAYER

Lord, You have given me the hidden key to Your heart and revealed the secret place of access to divine intimacy. Forgive me for my preoccupation with the opinions and approval of others when I should have eyes only for You. You tore down the dividing wall, and I will leave it there to run to the secret places of the stairs and commune with You.

Discover the Path of Secret Access and Tap the Power of Proximity

Somehow . . . five men developed a path of secret access to the heart of God. He is saying, "There are people whom I am reluctant to talk to in times like these because I know they can move My heart. They can bring Me to the point of doing something that was different from My original intention. It is as if some people can talk Me into more things than others can." We know it as the power of prayer!

THE GOD CATCHERS, P. 135

SCRIPTURE READING:

Ezekiel 14:14; Jeremiah 15:1; James 5:16, in which God speaks about five men who knew the path of secret access to His heart; and a New Testament exhortation about the power of prayer.

Some people scoff at the very idea of a mere man or woman moving the heart of God through fervent prayer. Perhaps in their understanding of things, everything that will ever happen is already written in stone, and we are mere pawns in the hands of uncaring fate. The problem with this idea is the holy book we call the Bible, with its outrageous revelation of the God who cared so much that He sent His only Son. To make matters more difficult for the theorists, that Book is filled with proof and testimony of divine intervention instigated by very, very human intercession and petition. As I stated in *The God Catchers*:

Explain to me why God singled out five men in the Old Testament the way He did. In the book of Ezekiel, God said: "Even if these three men, Noah, Daniel,

167

and Job, were in it, they would deliver only themselves by their righteousness. God also declared in the book of Jeremiah: "Even if Moses and Samuel stood before Me, My mind would not be favorable toward this people. Cast them out of My sight, and let them go forth." (pp. 134–35)

What is God saying in these passages? (*If you examine the context, it is clear that God is doing the talking.*) Would He say such a thing about you? (*Why not?*)

All of these men were certifiably human. They experienced serious adversity and hardships that they survived only through the personal intervention of God. There are two other traits they seemed to share: they were all incurable, chronic God Chasers, and they were personally involved in praying for and ministering to others. What made them stand out from the millions of people who also lived on this planet during their lifetimes?

These men managed to get close enough to God to win His heart in some way. This is the power of proximity personified. We are not talking about bribery or flattery; we are talking about God Chasers who knew how to pursue Him with genuine passion in ways that drew Him close. Noah, Daniel, Job, Moses, and Samuel—they all drew close to God in spite of impossible crises and adverse circumstances. (*The God Catchers,* p. 135)

What factors separate the power of proximity seen in the lives of these men from man's twisted imitations known as bribery and flattery? The first is the heart motive behind the words and actions; the second factor is relationship. My wife and children possess a special power of proximity with me because they are my family members, and I've given them the key to my heart. The third factor is God Himself. He is God, and He can be moved only when He chooses to be moved. He cannot be bribed or moved by flattery in any way. He has never received "offerings" given with impure motives, and He cannot be fooled or misled.

Do you long to draw near to Him because you love Him or because you love the blessings of His hand? How often do you approach Him

in love and adoration and make a petition on someone else's behalf instead of merely seeking your own good?

PRAYER

Father, I hunger and thirst for Your presence. Other things may satisfy the passing needs and desires of my physical body, but You alone are my total Source of joy, fulfillment, and abundant supply. I appreciate the bounty of Your hands, but I hunger for the beauty and grace revealed in Your face.

Building Habitations and Arks in a Scornful Land

What made Noah so special? The answer is that Noah chased God in a day when no one else on the planet cared whether or not God even existed, and he did it at great personal cost.

THE GOD CATCHERS, P. 135

SCRIPTURE READING:

Genesis 6:9–9:17, where we find the story of Noah, who dared to obey God although it made him look foolish and misled in the wisdom of men.

Worship takes many forms, and faith and obedience are two of the most prominent forms on the list. God is honored every time we dare to believe Him and trust Him with our lives and livelihood. He is also blessed when we obey Him even though we don't understand the purpose of His command or its final outcome.

How do you feel about obeying God before you know all of the details? Has He ever given His children all of the details before launching them on journeys of faith?

Noah is one of the five men God singled out as men of influence in heavenly matters precisely because he dared to believe and obey Him with very little confirmation and no human encouragement for nearly one hundred years.[2] How many modern God Chasers want to quit when they endure a week without encouragement from other believers?

How is your chase affected by the negative comments and disapproval of others? Are you influenced more by the criticism or by encouragement? What if you receive neither in the course of your chase for God?

What made Noah so special? What qualified him for inclusion among the faithful five who personified the power of proximity?

Noah continued to chase God in obedience despite universal disapproval of his God project. He endured the taunts, laughter, and nonstop verbal abuse of neighbors while he constructed a boat in a place with virtually no water and absolutely no rain! It was the equivalent of building an ocean liner in your backyard in the middle of the Mojave Desert, yet Noah did it and pleased God with his sacrifice of praise through obedience. In the end, Noah's righteousness and humility before God saved his entire family and the human race as well. (*The God Catchers,* pp. 135–36)

What can you learn from Noah's ark-building experience of the past that might help you build a habitation for God in the present?

Prayer

Father, sometimes I feel that I understand just a little of what Noah experienced because God Chasers aren't popular or accepted by many in the body of Christ or the unsaved world. You called us to radical commitment when You commanded us to deny ourselves every day and take our cross if we want to follow You.

I'm in hot pursuit of Your presence, and I refuse to slow down, quiet down, lie down, or give up the chase. I'm thankful for every visitation, but I'm determined to build a habitation of praise for You. In the meantime, just thirty seconds in Your presence will make it all worthwhile and energize me to resume the pursuit once again.

Perseverance to Pierce the Heavens

There was something about Daniel's hunger for God that brought instant response to his prayers. Maybe it was his appetite for heavenly wisdom or his humility before divinity that promoted him to the field of the five men whose words could capture the heart of God.

THE GOD CATCHERS, P. 137

SCRIPTURE READING:

Daniel 9:21–23; 10, where Daniel intercedes for his people, God quickly responds, and angels do battle on his behalf.

For thousands of years Christians and Jews alike have considered Daniel's name to be synonymous with prayer, conviction, and faith. God used Daniel's intercessory prayer for his people to illustrate the celestial operation of prayer and the nature of spiritual warfare in the heavenlies.

It is interesting that when the angel Gabriel appeared twenty-one days after Daniel began to pray and fast before God on behalf of his people, he said, "At the beginning of your supplications the command went out, and I have come to tell you, for you are greatly beloved."[3]

God answered Daniel's prayer on day one; the remaining twenty days were spent dealing with demonic hindrances to God's prompt response. I commented in *The God Catchers*, "The passages describing Daniel's intercession for his people reveal one of the Bible's clearest pictures of warfare in the heavenlies. It also shows how closely God listens to and heeds the prayers and cries of His people" (p. 136).

Daniel had the relationship and heart attitude that captured God's heart, but he also had the heart to persevere and overcome the adversary's resistance to God's will in the earth.

How do you compare to Daniel's godly standard of prayer and perseverance? Do you have the key to access God's heart? Do you have the determination, courage, and raw faith in God's faithfulness to keep praying even when you don't "feel" anything?

Leadership of any kind in the church usually operates on the iceberg principle. Most of the "work" of the ministry takes place in the hidden place of prayer and intimate communion with God. This creates the platform for the highly visible remainder of ministry that occurs in public view.

It seems that most of our ministry training efforts in traditional seminaries and schools of ministry focus on the public "tip of the iceberg" while minimizing or overlooking the all-important secret ministry of the prayer and worship closet that supports, energizes, and facilitates all public ministry.

Has anyone ever taught you how to persevere until you pierce the heavens? Are you prepared to experience it and then teach others how to do the same?

Daniel's life epitomized a life spent for God and for others. His life priorities were clear: he put his relationship and obedience to God first; then he served his people. He seemed to understand that God gave him favor with kings for a higher good than his personal comfort and security.

He consistently put God first above the approval of men and even above his own safety and comfort. He also realized that his privileged access to God was meant to benefit more than just himself. He had a responsibility to stand in the gap for others, exactly as another higher and greater Intercessor would one day stand in the gap of sin for the human race. (*The God Catchers*, p. 137)

For whom are you spending your life? Are you chasing Him with your praise, prayers, and worship for His sake? Are you investing

173

your power of proximity selflessly as an intercessor by standing in the gap on behalf of others?

PRAYER

Father, help me become the pursuer in prayer and the knight of the knees You ordained me to be. Teach me how to lay my life daily on the altar of surrender as I pursue Your face. Show me how to pray with the same passion, conviction, faith, and perseverance as Daniel so I may pierce the heavens and please You with my praise, worship, and fervent prayers of intercession.

In Passionate Pursuit of the Face Place

[Job] became God's "poster child for God Chasers" when he proved under extreme hardship that his love was directed to the Giver of blessings, not the blessings of the Giver.

THE GOD CATCHERS, P. 137

Perhaps Moses' secret point of access to the Father is revealed in this one-of-a-kind conversation with God: "So the Lord said to Moses, 'I will also do this thing that you have spoken; for you have found grace in My sight, and I know you by name.' *And he said, 'Please, show me Your glory.'"*

THE GOD CATCHERS, P. 139

SCRIPTURE READING:

Exodus 33:11–23, revealing the power of proximity in the relationship between Moses the God Chaser and God the Redeemer of men.

Two men in the Old Testament seem larger than life to us, even on this side of the Cross. We look at the lives of Job and Moses today and think, *Who in our day could do the things those men did in theirs?* Within the boundaries of God's purpose for your life, the answer is: you could.[4]

Job suffered while caught in the middle of a disagreement between the Creator and the fallen angel, Satan. That disagreement is still going on as you read this book, and it will continue until Satan is thrown into the lake of fire. Job lived long before Jesus entered the world in the form of a man, but in God's view, Satan had already been defeated by the Lamb "slain before the foundation of the world."[5] You live under the cloud of the same cosmic disagreement, and you have even greater benefits available to you from God's divine solution to sin. So what did Job do that you can do too?

> Job was a man who passed the supreme test of adversity and *demonstrated his unconditional love for God* before the galleries of both heaven and hell . . .
>
> Even though Job cried out in pain and often expressed his frustration and desperation through his ordeal, he never wavered in his unqualified love for God. (*The God Catchers,* p. 137, italics mine)

How do you bear the pain of adversity or of being misunderstood by your friends? Do you still chase God when the sky seems to fall on your head, or do you shake your fist at heaven in anger and resentment? Is your love for Him truly unconditional?

What was so special about Moses? Once again we discover a murderer transformed by a life-changing encounter with the manifest presence of God. Moses, like Saul centuries later, was formally trained for leadership but misused his authority and zeal until God intervened. Understanding this should give all of us hope. What was this man's secret ?

MOSES: GOD KNEW HIM BY NAME

> The murderer and picture of failure God chose to deliver His people was no stranger to God's anointing and glory. Time and again, we see Moses spending long periods of time in God's smoke-obscured presence receiving the Ten Commandments, the Law, and the detailed instructions for the tabernacle of Moses and the ark of the covenant. (*The God Catchers,* p. 138)

How much time do you spend alone with God? Would you say that the fruit or end product of your life in God might increase if you increase the amount of time you invest in your relationship and communion with the Deity?

Perhaps most important of all, Moses was the one man who dared to ask for the impossible in his passion for God. He asked God to show him His face.

He had to wait 1,500 years and pass from life to death to see it come to pass,[6] but he was an incurable God Chaser with a passion for God that would not be limited by the less passionate masses around him.

As I wrote in *The God Chasers,* "This burning desire to see God's glory, to see Him face to face, is one of the most important keys to revival, reformation, and the fulfillment of God's purposes on the earth."[7]

Do you have a burning desire in your life? Do you burn to see His face and dwell in His presence, or do you burn for more earthly issues and concerns? How do you feel about passion and the radical pursuit of God? Is it worth living and dying for?

PRAYER

Father, I'm desperate for the face place, the place of divine encounter where my humanity encounters Your divinity and falls down in complete and unconditional surrender and love. Lord, show me Your face.

Touch His Heart, Change Your World

[Samuel's] relationship with God was so unique in that spiritually dry era that the Scriptures say, "So Samuel grew, and the Lord was with him and let none of his words fall to the ground."[8] *How many of us can make that claim today? This God Catcher knew how to touch the heart of God and change his world.*

THE GOD CATCHERS, P. 139

SCRIPTURE READING:

1 Samuel 1–3, where the early history of Samuel's miraculous birth and timely calling are described in vivid and passionate detail.

Many great church leaders share a common bond with Samuel, the Old Testament prophet who anointed young David as the future king of Israel. His ministry was birthed before his conception in the passionate, brokenhearted prayers of his mother.

One man in the list of five is literally named "Heard of God," and his life and ministry epitomized his name. Samuel's very conception and birth came about because his mother's desperate cry was "heard of God."[9]

In a day when few people heard from God, one desperate woman named Hannah touched the heart of God by ignoring the protests of the religious elite and crossing the gender and religious barriers erected by a dim-sighted priesthood. Her tears and utter desperation broke through the brass heavens and brought to birth the prophet who eventually anointed and guided King David.[10] Evidently she imparted her anointing to Samuel, who took it to another level. (*The God Catchers*, p. 139)

What is your desperation level? Do you dream big enough and love deep enough to birth a miracle through passionate prayer? Will you brave the disapproval of the dispassionate to carry God's dream to full term in your life?

We do the kingdom a grave disservice when we impose artificial limits upon those who would obey God and lay down their lives in His service. To some we say, "You are too young." To others we shake our heads in dismissal and say, "You are too old." We use whatever brand of wet blanket it takes to put out the fire, whether it is the blanket of gender, generational, or educational prejudice. God uses anyone who dares to say yes when He calls.

The Bible says Samuel served the Lord in a linen priest's ephod even at a young age, and he learned to hear God's still small voice as a young boy in the temple. He never forgot how to listen to and serve divinity. (*The God Catchers,* p. 139)

What would happen today if young Samuel or his desperate mother showed up at the doorstep of your home or church? What if God asks you to weep before Him in such desperation that it attracts the disapproval of others who do not understand? What if He calls you in the night hours in a voice you've never heard before?

PRAYER

Lord, I feel like an orphan of faith, like one eternally lent to the Lord and brought to birth for a life of service in Your presence. I am a bond servant of love joyfully abandoned at the door of Your house, and I won't be happy anywhere else. Take me into Your presence; teach Me to hear Your voice, touch Your heart, and speak Your words to my generation.

Discover the Secret Access to the Celestial "Yes"

The five men seemingly hand selected by God in the Old Testament era seemed to know about and understand what Solomon called "the secret of the stairs." The men knew this secret "back stairs" access to God's presence could produce a celestial "yes" when every earthly circumstance said "no."

THE GOD CATCHERS, P. 140

SCRIPTURE READING:

Matthew 7:7–11, where Jesus teaches vital principles of fervent prayer offered to the Father as family members, which were first unveiled through the lives of Old Testament men.

Some bad habits and wrong ideas are hard to kill. I see evidence that countless numbers of Christians still cling to the "God is in heaven with a baseball bat" view of the heavenly Father. As a result, they easily dismiss decades of Bible teaching and every example of God's goodness in their lives to cling to their belief that God doesn't really love them. This unconscious conviction is a faith-destroying cancer that preempts the very idea of God Chasing and invalidates nearly every attempt at prayer.

Has your life or the lives of loved ones been touched by this disease of the discarded? How have you dealt with it (if you have)?

We often act as if we are convinced that God merely puts up with us while constantly monitoring our conduct with baseball bat in hand (just in case we make a mistake or commit a sin). Nothing could be farther from the truth. It is true that God is righteous and that He hates sin, but He loves us so much that He gave His own Son to die so that we might live.[11] Jesus painted a totally different picture of the Father when He said, "If you then, being evil, know how to give good gifts to your children, how much more will your Father who is in heaven give good things to those who ask Him!"[12]

> Passionate worship will weave its way through the trappings of failure, discouragement, and difficulty to bring you to the place of passion with Him.
>
> This is what it means to "worship until you get to the face place" or to "tarry until . . ." You refuse to stop or turn aside to celebrate when His hand of blessing "sticks out from underneath the veil." You are after more than the blessings of His hands; you want the glory of His face. You've made up your mind and refined your pursuit to the point that you no longer seek a blessing; you are after nothing less than the Blesser. (*The God Catchers*, pp. 140–41)

Will you discard every picture of God in your heart and mind that fails to match His portrait in God's Word? Are you prepared to allow the Holy Spirit to remodel your prayer model? Will you approach Him as your loving heavenly Father instead of a distant cosmic caretaker who cares nothing for you?

Love brought Jesus to earth in the form of a helpless baby. Love and joy led Him to endure the pain and suffering of the cross for us, and love led God to give us the secret of the stairs, the secret door of access into His presence.[13]

The men of old who knew how to touch God's heart learned then what we are discovering now: we often think God is waiting to say no when He really longs to say yes. The secret to the celestial "yes" is to seek His face and not merely His hands.

> If you are not in this place now, it is certain that someday you will be asking the Father for things that logic says are impossible: "That can't be revived. There is no way that can be taken care of. Don't you know you can't do this, and that request is out of the question?" At the same time, passion is saying, "I think I know a way.

There is a back door, a secret stairway that can lead you there, but the only way to reach it is through passionate worship." (*The God Catchers,* p. 143)

Are you convinced that God loves you? Are you tapping the secret of the celestial "yes" by pursuing the glory of His face more than the blessings of His hands? When you do offer petitions to the Father, do you take care to ask in accordance with His will rather than yours?[14]

Once you allow the Word of God to establish the banks or boundaries of the river, you must yield to the flow of the Spirit in your life. We know that God never acts or operates outside the principles He established in His Word; but we should equally understand that God still speaks and leads His people today. If He doesn't, then why did Jesus, the apostles, and all of the inspired New Testament writers even bother to command us to pray (which they did often)?[15]

Obviously no one can or should even try to manipulate God to do something. However, it is also obvious to me that God "sets us up" for fresh encounters and gives us the "secret of the stairs" just to intensify and preserve our dependence upon and passion for Him. (*The God Catchers,* p. 143)

PRAYER

Father, thank You for revealing the secret of the stairs to the church and Your children. Teach me how to pray the effectual, fervent prayer of the righteous and tap the power of the celestial "yes." Your Word commands me to pray, and it is my delight to seek Your face and pray until Your will is done on earth as it is in heaven. I'm desperate for You; therefore, I will seek You with all of my heart, mind, soul, and strength.

I Want You, Daddy!

The Cry God Can't Deny

God does not hide so that He can't be found; He hides so that He can be found. In good times we tend to seek Him too casually, as if we don't really need His help.

It is in those moments that we begin to sense His conspicuous absence from our day-to-day routines and rituals. If we are wise, we begin to cultivate our hunger anew. If we are foolish, we grow hardened and accustomed to the absence of His manifest presence, as if it doesn't matter.

In the hard times, when we are helpless, lost, and feel totally unable to find Him in our pain; when the only cry we can offer Him is an urgent plea of desperation or a sharp cry of pain, He comes suddenly in answer to the cry He can't deny.

God Prefers the Simple Passion of Desperation Over the Grandiose Prayers of Lofty Religion

Verbal eloquence is no match for the simple passion of a baby's cry, or the passionate plea of a broken and desperate heart. Grandiose prayers in the best seventeenth-century "King James" English could not begin to match the sheer passion of Ishmael's cry that day.

THE GOD CATCHERS, P. 147

SCRIPTURE READING:

Genesis 21:8–20, where God hears Ishmael's passionate cries and decreed his destiny.

Despite nearly two thousand years of linguistic research, biblical scholarship, and church history, the church still seems to have a habit of misreading or purposely ignoring Bible passages referring to the heart, the center of man's spiritual and emotional being.

"Surely those first-century writers were culturally misled and truly mistaken," we say. "Truly spiritual people know there is no virtue in serving God with the emotions." Perhaps the greatest offender among the New Testament verses is called the Great Commandment by Jews and Christians alike. You can probably recite it by heart: "You shall love the LORD your God with all your heart, with all your soul, and with all your mind."[1]

Intellectual pursuits have little to do with God Chasing. I am a lifelong student of great literature, analytical thought, and conceptual theory. I believe that God has a universe of complexity worthy of intense intellectual study and appreciation, but I know that intellectual appreciation of a body of data about God will never lead you to lay down your life and agenda to pursue Him with total abandon. That is a matter of passionate love—not logic—and it certainly includes the emotions.

Have you ever been taught that emotions are totally bad or second-rate components of your being? Have you ever considered passion to be a word unworthy of your Christian faith (except when referring to the Lord's passion)? What do you believe (keeping the Great Commandment in mind)?

The problem with human intellect is its close relationship with human pride. I read somewhere that "knowledge puffs up."[2] We have a habit of believing we can control anything once we think we understand it. Human theologians "progressed" from the reverent study of God's Word and character to endless arguments over obtuse linguistic points.

Human intellectual pursuit of God really came of age late in the nineteenth century when theologians began second-guessing the Divine Record to the point that a leading German theologian named Friedrich Wilhelm Nietzsche confidently announced to the world, "God is dead."[3]

Nietzsche suffered a mental breakdown in 1889 and died in 1900, evidently unaware that no one told God He was supposed to be dead too. Knowledge puffs up, but love builds up.

Nietzsche taught that traditional Christians are weak and resentful slaves in bondage to an outmoded concept of God. As a God Chaser, are you eager to display your weakness and dependence upon God, or do you struggle to hide your God addiction to please people who act as if God is dead?

Have you noticed how quickly pride settles in once you start to feel good about some newly acquired knowledge in God's Word? There is nothing wrong with academic studies or accomplishments as long as your heart motives are right, but have you ever felt the pull and desire to accumulate academic degrees to win the approval of men?

There's nothing like the real thing arriving to make the counterfeit apparent.

It took only a few years for Abraham's house to become too small to hold two "sons of promise" at the same time. Hagar and Ishmael were given a small amount of food and water and sent into the desert. Before long, the water ran out and so did hope. Hagar put her crying teenage son under a bush and moved out of earshot, praying that the Lord wouldn't let her see her son die. Then the Bible says: "And God heard the voice of the lad. Then the angel of God called to Hagar out of heaven, and said to her, 'What ails you, Hagar? Fear not, for God has heard the voice of the lad where he is.'" (*The God Catchers,* p. 147)

God heard the voice of a desperate teenager in a Middle Eastern desert. Would He hear your desperate voice today? Would you characterize yourself as a Hagar hiding and distancing yourself from emotional pain while complaining to God, or as an Ishmael voicing your desperation directly to God? Which one would God hear or answer first?

The human race must have an unconscious attraction to eloquence. The comparison between verbal eloquence and simple passion reminds me of the choice Samuel the prophet faced the day Jesse the shepherd lined up his sons for an anointing service. Samuel was about to anoint Jesse's oldest boy, a tall man with the look of a leader and the appearance of boldness about him—then God interrupted him for another theology lesson. He said, "Do not look at his appearance or at the height of his stature, because I have refused him. For the LORD does not see as man sees; for man looks at the outward appearance, but the LORD looks at the heart."[4]

Eloquence can't be equated with automatic response! (*The God Catchers,* p. 147)

Prayer

Father, please forgive me for the times I've become puffed up with pride, and for the times I've been reluctant to display my passion for You because other people were watching. The truth is that I am desperate for You; I long for Your presence, and my addiction to Your glory is growing. Give me the courage and grace to boldly seek Your face before men and angels, no matter what the circumstances.

How to Tap an Infinitely Renewable Energy Source

If the determinate length of our waiting actually predetermines the size and passion of His answer, then perhaps that explains why true revival has evaded most of the church. We know that passion will cause the heart of the Father to do things that otherwise He wouldn't do, but holy desperation may even move Him more!

THE GOD CATCHERS, P. 149

SCRIPTURE READING:

Isaiah 40:28–31, where the prophet describes all of the benefits received by those who learn how to wait upon the Lord.

In the passage from Isaiah, why did God use the word *wait*? If you think about it, the closest thing we have to a "god in a hurry" is the prideful angel who pretended to be God and was ushered out of heaven in a hurry. The true God is never in a hurry, and He is never late. If anything, time bends to match His pace, not the other way around.

The closest thing to rushing we should experience is the rush to kneel before Him when He manifests His glory among us and the rush to obey His commands. In these situations, tardiness may indicate a weakness of love or a lack of wisdom. Any other hurrying may indicate our schedule is out of control or even under the subtle influence or driving pressure of the would-be god in a hurry known as the adversary.

What is the pace of your prayer and worship life? Do you rush through your worship and prayer times and then anxiously await an immediate reply? Why is it important to wait on God when seeking His face for a long-term visitation?

If our waiting upon Divinity has value in God's eyes, perhaps our passion for Him has an even greater impact on His heart. In *The God Catchers*, I referred to the children of Israel suffering under Egyptian bondage in the Old Testament and noted:

Yet the day came when things got so bad that the people uttered a different kind of cry. This cry had a cutting edge of desperation that possessed the power to cut through the brassy heavens over Egypt and capture the heart of God! That was when He allowed Moses to "catch" Him at the burning bush and announced, *"I heard their cry,* so I came down to deliver them out and bring them up."

The people of God had stumbled upon another secret key in their desperation that unlocked the heart of divinity and made heaven invade their hell. (p. 148)

Have you ever stumbled across the secret key of desperate prayer from the heart, only to be surprised by the swiftness and power of God's reply? Was it manipulation on your part or anticipation of the Divinity to answer your cry and meet your need?

Persistence is one of the legitimate forms of waiting on God. Many believers in previous generations called it "praying through." Isaiah the prophet called it "waiting on God." Most of us today who have experienced it call it a combination of pure desperation, dogged determination, and holy perspiration.

The widow used this tool to unlock the hardened will of the heartless judge in Jesus' parable to the disciples.[5] It is the bombshell of a broken heart that Hannah unleashed on heaven from the dim chambers of the tabernacle where Eli the priest presided.[6] It is the essence of the High Priestly Prayer that Jesus poured out to heaven as a drink offering of desperation, sacrifice, and obedience to the Father in the face of death.[7] It is the cry God cannot deny.

Have you ever persevered in prayer until heaven came down to earth? Are you prepared to pray until the foundations of your prison shake and every chain encircling your neighborhood just drops away? Will you become a persistent Hannah on behalf of a nation in need of deliverance? (You may have to pray until the unexpected fires of revival are ignited—and then give it all back to God without taking the credit.)

I believe there are unused keys of power and divine access lying on the dusty shelves of the church that we have forgotten about. Desperate passion of worship or the painful cries of crisis are going to unlock the heavens for somebody . . .

Frankly it is uncommon for the modern church to press through to this level of divine access. Perhaps it is because a good number of us can barely stomach a seventy-minute prayer meeting, much less a seven- or ten-day interval of intense prayer, worship, or fasting (as when the 120 "tarried" for the Holy Spirit in the Upper Room in the book of Acts). (*The God Catchers*, p. 149)

PRAYER

Lord, teach me the power of the "press," the determination and desire that will take me past the veil and into Your presence. Help me to tarry, wait, persist, and stand in the prayer of faith and the worship of desperation until heaven comes down and Your glory is revealed.

Whether You Come to Him or He Comes to You, Brokenness Is the Link Between Heaven and Earth

Sometimes you come in your fullness and make yourself empty, as Zacchaeus did. At other times you cry out in your bankruptcy, hunger, and pain, and God shows up. That's the cry God can't deny.

THE GOD CATCHERS, P. 149

SCRIPTURE READING:

Psalm 51:16–17, where David desperately asks God for forgiveness after his adultery with Bathsheba and the murder of her husband—and discovers the power of genuine repentance and a broken and contrite heart.

Men and women come to Him in every conceivable posture and position, but we all wind up in the same position in the end—on bended knee.

Some come to Him steeped in pride and stiffened by a stubbornness descended from Adam's seed.

Others bend low and come to Him in the knowledge of their sin, and some come crawling facedown in their desperate need for deliverance, healing, and miraculous intervention in their impossible situations. It seems easier for God to lift someone who comes to Him meek and lowly than to "lower" someone who comes to His throne haughtily.

How do you approach the King of glory—from the position of the meek and lowly or from the position of pride while parading your

own strength? Do you cast your prayer list at His feet, or do you first throw your crown at His feet in worship, humility, and unconditional adoration?

I pray that the church will arise and seek the face of the Reviver with such unity that He will come suddenly to reveal His glory. If it happens, then (to rephrase my statement from *The God Catchers,* p. 151) "His heart won't change because of our impeccably structured request or the sheer logic of our arguments. Logic won't have anything to do with it, but passion and relationship had *everything* to do with it."

> Passion caused God to remodel heaven so He could turn the dead-end door of death into a secret place of access to heaven. In His passion He said, "I have to figure out a way to get My kids in here, even if I have to remodel what was pre-existent." *It is illogical that God would sacrifice His own Son just to get close to you, but passion got in His way.* (*The God Catchers,* pp. 151–52)

Many people would love to challenge the very concept of passion in the church by asking, "What does passion have to do with the gospel?" Passion has everything to do with it.

Pure logic would rule out the mercy and grace Jesus made possible on the cross. It was passion that led God to sacrifice so much for what seems to be so little in heaven's economy. The Bible says, "For God so loved . . ."—not "For God so thought . . ."[8] I am not against logical thought or the acquisition of knowledge; but I must protest when I see logic, human thought, and mere knowledge exalted to idol status.

What role does God-ward passion play in your life? Do you pursue Him primarily because it seems logical or because passion for His presence leaves you no choice?

It is . . . the passion of a God Chaser that transforms him into a God Catcher. (*The God Catchers,* p. 152)

PRAYER

Father, I am consumed with hunger for Your presence. Show me how to empty myself when necessary to receive Your fullness. In those times when I feel empty and weary, teach me how to turn the tables on trouble by offering my emptiness to You in exchange for the joy and refreshment of Your presence.[9]

Press Beyond Casual Hunger for the Ultimate Reward of Passionate Desperation

Perhaps you have gone beyond the stage of casual hunger. You have even surpassed the supercharged arena of hunger fueled by passion. You have reached the point of all-out desperation where you no longer act like yourself. You are desperate for an encounter at the face place. Hunger is written all over your face. You have become like Moses who said, in essence, "I'm tired of Your hands; show me Your face, Lord. Show me Your glory."

THE GOD CATCHERS, P. 153

SCRIPTURE READING:

Matthew 13:14–17, the chilling explanation Jesus provided for Isaiah's prophecy about those with eyes that do not see and ears that do not hear (the casual nibblers)—all sandwiched between the teaching on Jonah's experience of reluctant obedience and the parable of the sower.

Casual hunger is a sign of lethargy and inactivity. With few exceptions I've noticed that when people tackle labor-intensive tasks or projects that push them beyond their normal limits, they get hungry—really hungry. Our bodies burn energy when we work, play, or think with intensity. They store excess energy in the form of fat when inactivity takes over.

How would you describe the modern church: lethargic and over-weight, or energetic and ravenously hungry? How would you describe your personal walk with God?

Casual Christianity may actually be our worst enemy in this millennium. As I observed in *The God Catchers:*

> After centuries of painting passion as something evil and untrustworthy, the church must rediscover the true power of "God-ward passion." I read somewhere that God's Son exhibited His uninhibited passion for His Father's house: "Zeal for Your house has eaten Me up." Pardon me, but that doesn't sound very laid-back or logical to me. It sounds radical, illogical, and "over the edge" of proper religious behavior. (p. 152)

When was the last time something happened in your local church service that was passionate, uninhibited, zealous, radical, illogical, or even "over the edge"? Are you ready to follow His footsteps and allow yourself to be "eaten up" by zeal for the Father's house?

Perhaps the reason so many in the body of Christ avoid the passion of the face place is that they fear the responsibility that comes with divine encounter. We never leave such an encounter unchanged because it is about impartation more than information transfer. When God plants His desire in a human heart, a divine transaction takes place involving empowerment, vision, and a godly determination beyond the norm. This much is sure: you will think and act differently afterward.

> It takes only thirty seconds in the manifest presence of God to change the course of history for you, your city, or the nation. There is a river of tears rising across America and the world right now. This flood of holy hunger has been orchestrated by God Himself. He is determined to prepare places of divine encounter, but it is up to us to "climb the tree of destiny." (*The God Catchers*, p. 153)

Has the level of hunger in your heart been rising? Have you noticed anything strange taking place in your church or in other churches across the nation and the world? What are you prepared to do about it? Are you really prepared for the life change that comes with a God encounter at the face place?

You need to put your hunger on display like a little child who is totally oblivious to the satisfied and settled people around you. Put a voice to your God-induced hunger and pain. It is time to run to the "face place" for a one-on-one encounter with your heavenly Father. Expect God to answer when you pray, "Father, set our hearts on fire with passion." (*The God Catchers*, pp. 153–54)

PRAYER

Father, set my heart on fire with passion for Your presence. May every other request, petition, and complaint fall behind the deepest cry of my heart: I want You, Daddy!

Enter His Presence with Your Words, Leave It with a Depository of His Divine Purpose

When the Scriptures say we must become as little children to come to Him, it is God's way of saying, "You will always be My baby." He is always ready to play another round of celestial hidey-face with His children.

The beckoning finger of God is saying, "Come on." It is time to put a demand on the passion of God . . . You have no idea how much He loves you. Let your worship and hunger cry out to Him in desperation right now.

THE GOD CATCHERS, P. 155

SCRIPTURE READING:

Hosea 14, where the prophet urges the children of Israel to repent and return to the Lord, taking words with them.

It was customary in ancient times for anyone having an audience with a king to bring gifts with him. We must revive that custom in the church.

In most so-called worship services we offer the King of kings only a few halfhearted songs sung mostly for ourselves and some partial tithes and offerings (some of which are laced with the offensive smell of grudging resentment or doubt and unbelief).

But for the grace and mercy of God, we would all be dead by now. Perhaps that explains why too many American Christians seem to demonstrate more passion over a basketball referee's call than over the eternal things of God.

What do you offer the God who made everything? Your works are valued, but do they have any value to Him? How do you open the heart of the King of kings?

Never come before the King "empty-mouthed." Bring Him the treasures of your heart carefully wrapped and delivered in the passionate words of your lips—a sacrifice of praise and thanksgiving. Words can run faster than works; worship will capture what your hands can't reach.

Your works will never capture Him, but your worship, your passion, and your cry of desperation will capture His heart and usher in His presence when nothing else can.

Some of us need to make a "nagging phone call to Daddy" right now and say, "Daddy, I want You." It doesn't matter whether we kneel, stand, or lie prostrate on the floor. Any posture is appropriate in the passionate pursuit of His presence. (*The God Catchers*, p. 154)

How will you enter His presence the next time you seek Him? Where is your greatest passion in life? Are you prepared to live the rest of your life as a child in His presence?

The process begins with a simple cry of the heart, a longing of the soul given voice through your conscious choice. You may be reluctant to start because you make things more difficult than they really are. There are no formulas, programs, or seven-step plans to His presence, but there are truthfulness, repentance, and the words of your heart.

Just be prepared for Him to answer your cry. It happens so rarely in the environment of religion and hypocrisy that many of us are shocked when God actually answers us! (I would rather be shocked than not.)

I must warn you again that once you begin the progression of frustration, you can never return to "life as usual." It's a lot like getting pregnant. Once it happens, nothing will ever be the same. The heavens are pregnant with purpose right now because God is preparing to birth something. Men and women everywhere are saying they feel "awkward, off balance, and strangely out of place."

This ungainly awkwardness of man is typical when God prepares to arrive on the scene. (*The God Catchers*, p. 155)

PRAYER

There's no turning back now, Lord. It's too late for me. I've fallen for You, and I can't get enough of You any other way. I'm desperate for an encounter with You, for an all-out surrender at the face place that leaves me delightfully and permanently addicted to You. If my life becomes a depository for divine purpose, so be it. I'll carry Your dream to full term just for the privilege of seeing Your face.

Desperate to Deliver Something Larger than Ourselves

A woman in labor has gone beyond the definition of hunger and far surpassed the meaning of passion. Now she is openly, unapologetically desperate to deliver her gift to the world. So it is with the people of God at the apex of the progression of divine frustration.

THE GOD CATCHERS, P. 159

SCRIPTURE READING:

Romans 8:18–23, where we are told "the whole creation groans and labors with birth pangs together until now" in a picture that perfectly describes the condition of the church today.

The time of mystery is over, and the news is out: the church is pregnant, and something big is coming soon. Parts of the body have lodged protests over the inconvenience and impropriety of the whole thing, but it is too late. God is about to birth something in the earth through His bride that will affect the nations. We shouldn't be surprised to see our lives disrupted.

People in every era and culture understand what happens to a woman who is nearly full term in her pregnancy. Her center of gravity has drastically changed, her balance has shifted, and she is forced to walk differently. This perfectly describes the church today. It feels off balance and awkward right now. Why? The church is pregnant with the purposes of God and the time of birth is near.

. . . If the determinate length of our waiting really does predetermine the size and passion of His answer, then perhaps it would help to apply this concept to our "divine pregnancy." I heard somewhere that the pregnancy of an elephant lasts two years! Perhaps that means that the "larger births" are always preceded by the longest gestation periods. (*The God Catchers*, p. 156)

Do you feel spiritually off balance and stretched at times? Is there an expectancy in your spirit that keeps growing stronger with every hint of His nearness and every rumor of His visitation?

Don't be surprised if His sudden visitation throws you off even more. God usually "births" things in individual hearts before He touches entire regions as a whole because He always uses people who yield to Him to carry change and revival to the world.

Consider examples of God's dealings with women in the Bible. When He touched Sarah's barren and aged womb, she became pregnant and gave birth to Isaac.[10] When He touched Rebekah, she became pregnant with twins and bore Jacob and Esau.[11]

The angel of the Lord touched Manoah's wife, and she became pregnant and bore Samson, who would judge Israel.[12] When God answered the desperate prayer of a barren woman named Hannah, she became pregnant and gave birth to Samuel.[13] He touched a priest named Zacharias, and his barren wife, Elizabeth, became pregnant with John the Baptist.[14] Finally, when the Holy Spirit touched Mary, she became pregnant with Jesus.[15]

Do you really want God to touch you? Are you prepared for the changes, the stretching, the frustration, the public scrutiny, and the hard work of labor that come with pregnancy?

When the "fullness of time" comes, when something is about to be born into the world, all of the pressure and expectancy of the pregnancy comes to bear on one goal—the safe delivery of the new into the old. Until that moment, we may feel that time has nearly stopped along the way.

Do you feel as if you've been pregnant with the promises of God for a long time? You have done everything you know to do to bring it to pass, and now it has brought you to your knees and you are desperate. You have finally arrived in the ultimate posture of worship—desperate despondency! (*The God Catchers,* p. 157)

Are you weary with the chase? Do you feel discouraged because the time you've spent waiting on Him has outstripped your memory of the moments you spent in His presence?

Once a holy thing is birthed in your life or church, it may take you the rest of your life or many generations of the church family to catch up to the inner work God completed in you in just moments. Consider Saul, who was renamed Paul:

He met the resurrected Carpenter from Galilee, and it took three years of isolation in the desert for Paul's theology to catch up with his thirty-second experience with the Messiah in blinding glory.[16] He poured out this revelation knowledge in the form of New Testament letters or epistles he wrote to the young churches in the first century. We are still feasting on the revelation knowledge Paul received in that thirty-second moment of time. (*The God Catchers,* pp. 157–58)

Have you ever experienced an encounter with the resurrected Carpenter that left your life spinning and made your old life and ministry obsolete? How did He impart His heart to you? Did He work through your intellect or speak directly to your heart, leaving the intellect to catch up later?

Prayer

Father, I don't understand everything You've done in my heart, and I don't need to. I just know how desperate I am to see Your face and introduce others to the same joy. You've ruined me for every form and product of man-centered religion. I long to pursue Your presence and do Your will.

Whatever You imparted to me is greater than I am, and it is more difficult to accomplish or deliver than all of my talents, energies, abilities, and faith put together. The only solution is to stay close to You until Your purposes in my life come to pass.

Daddy, I Want You! (In Good Times and in Bad)

Don't get weary in your waiting. You are too close and too far along to back out now. Don't stop—maybe this is what it looks like right before the heavens break and He emerges through the matrix of time to manifest His glory among us.

If you are waiting on a promise from God, fan the flames of your desperation and put it on display. Make that nagging phone call to heaven and tell Him, "Daddy, I want You!"

THE GOD CATCHERS, P. 160

SCRIPTURE READING:

Psalm 126:5–6, in which tearful sowers are encouraged and chronic seed bearers are assured of a harvest.

Nearly every meeting I attend (and I lost track long ago), I tell myself, *Maybe this is the night He will come. Maybe this is the day He will reveal Himself once again.* Sometimes I get weary, but most of my fatigue stems from impatience with "man things."

Frankly I'm hungry for Him, not for His earthly assistants. I love the people of God, complete with all of their oddities, differences, and special quirks. The only thing for which I have no patience is the stuff of humanity posing as the stuff of Divinity. When I'm hungry for Him and His, nothing else will do.

Are you weary with empty religion and man-produced revival? Are you afraid you will end the chase just before God shows up? (You should be; He is close to you if you are really desperate.)

Worship is the process where we find Him in our wholeness. Brokenness is the process whereby God finds us in pieces. I am convinced that God hides when we think nothing is wrong, just to preserve the freshness of encounter. We are in our most dangerous state when we think everything is fine and we are "satisfied" with life. (*The God Catchers*, pp. 160–61)

The Bible says even the rocks and trees will cry out to God if we don't. What is so special about humanity's worship that draws Divinity close? For one thing, we don't have to do it. Our worship is really special when we finally come to our senses and offer Him what we were created to give Him— freely given worship offered in spirit and in truth.

True worship can be offered only from a humble heart consumed with love for Him. That is what makes your worship special in the times when you are relatively "whole" and everything seems to be fine. It is worship precisely because you choose to take your eyes off yourself and your wants long enough to acknowledge that He is the center of your universe. He is the Creator and you are His creation; and you love Him simply because He is.

Do you find the pace of your chase slowing down when things seem to be going well in your life? To put it another way, do you pursue Him with more passion and urgency when things are going wrong in your life? How can you step up the pace of the pursuit even during the good times?

For better or for worse, most of us find it easier or more natural to pursue God's face with fresh passion during difficult times. Perhaps it is part of our nature, or maybe God designed it that way knowing we would face regular challenges in our daily lives. Either way, life is always better when we're "following hard after God" than when we chase our own fleeting dreams and fantasies apart from Him.

God has no need to "hide" from us in our times of crises or self-cultivated hunger. When we fall into sin and hurt ourselves or grow desperately frustrated during the pursuit, God immediately shows up. The game is up because *the purpose of joy is discovery, not the chase itself.*

For the same reason, the Father takes joy in transforming God Chasers into God Catchers. He likes to let you catch Him! *The purpose of the pursuit is the finding, not the hiding,* and nothing changes the hiding into the finding so quickly as the cry God can't deny. (*The God Catchers,* p. 161, italics mine)

How do you cultivate hunger for Him in good times? Do you make a daily habit of reading His letters, remembering the joy of His presence, and lingering over every memory of His faithfulness in your life and the lives of others? Does this process sound similar to the patterns we often follow in human relationships?

Prayer

Father, I miss You. Thanks to Your favor and faithfulness, things go right in my life much of the time. In the bad times, when my life, my health, my family members, or my financial security is threatened by the circumstances of life, I have no problem running to You. That is when I struggle to hold the course until You come.

It is in the good times that I most often fail to seek You with passion and urgency. The truth is that I am always in a crisis apart from Your presence. I need You moment by moment. I long for Your presence every minute of my life and beyond. Keep me desperately hungry and passionate for You, Lord; and lead me not into the temptation of satisfaction and dullness of heart.

Living in the Village of Repentance at Frustration's Address

(And Content to Stay There)

If the ideal tranquil life of a Christian inspires images of you and Jesus floating on the serene waters of a crystal sea, then the God Chaser's life more closely resembles the adventures of Peter, who accepted the Lord's challenge to step out of the boat of apparent comfort into the chaos of the churning sea in the middle of a storm.

We must be willing to pursue Him in any circumstance or situation, armed and motivated solely by the strength of His Word and our passion to be in His presence.

It seems the tranquil life may be a fruitless life as well. The tranquillity of God is most often found in the eye of the storm. That is where God Chasers finally become God Catchers; it is where humanity takes the hand of the Deity for a miraculous walk across the waters of impossibility to the sure ground of God's purposes.

Holy Filling Is the Quest,
Holy Frustration Is the Address

"But, Tommy, I don't like living with this . . . this, this uneasy feeling. Will I ever stop feeling that I need more of Him?"

Will it help if I tell you that all the spiritual luminaries of ages past have lived at frustration's address? Holy Hunger is their street in the village of Repentance, and Divine Desperation is their zip code. Their hunger was greater than their receiving, and their divine discontent made them pray a prayer like this: "Show me Your glory." They didn't base their faith on the success of their pursuit; they based their pursuit on the strength of their faith.

THE GOD CATCHERS, P. 164

SCRIPTURE READING:

2 Corinthians 11:23–12:12, where Paul portrays the "glamorous" life of a first-century apostle and describes what it was like to live at frustration's address while glorying only in his weaknesses and his total dependence upon God's strength.

The myth persists that we enjoy a perfect life after receiving Christ despite two millennia of persecution, adversity, and opposition for His name. The lives of Peter, Paul, James, John, and many other less known saints mentioned in the Bible make it clear that divine desperation is a natural part of our life in Christ.

Some may hope it isn't so, but students of the Word *know* it's so. God Chasers who hope to become God Catchers must inevitably enter the zip code of Divine Desperation and take up residence in the village of Repentance. In their quest for holy filling, they make their home on the street of Holy Hunger.

Is your hunger greater than your receiving? Do you know what it feels like to experience His presence and yet hunger for more?

The passionate pursuit of God's presence puts a serious demand on the human soul, a price that some may find too high to pay. As I noted in *The God Catchers:*

Once you decide to abandon your permanent place in the pew or leave that comfortable padded seat in the back of the church to chase Him, God issues a permanent change-of-address notice for you. From that moment on, you become a spiritual traveler in transit, a pilgrim on an eternal pilgrimage to the place of His presence.[1] (p. 164)

The necessity of repentance is the first demand you encounter when you enter the chase. It dawns on you that the repentance that led to salvation was a door to deeper repentance, not just a onetime occurrence. From that point on, salvation is not the issue that has been accomplished for you by Christ Jesus. Now you are consumed with a desire for holiness and righteousness before the One you long to be near, and a broken and repentant heart is the first stepping-stone to His manifest presence.

Are you prepared to live life as a spiritual pilgrim in perpetual pursuit of His presence? Were you ever told about the importance of repentance—continual repentance—to those who hunger for righteousness and holiness?

Repentance can accelerate the process of entering His presence. I've often said that repentance is like "worship on steroids." True repentance produces godly sorrow that bridges the gap of sin that separates us from Him. It also births desperation and brokenness.

If worship entreats the presence of God, it seems that repentance places a demand on His presence because He said He will not despise the sacrificial cry of a broken and repentant heart.[2]

. . . The full faith of God Himself backs His statement about repentance. It places a legitimate demand on His presence; it fuels it like pressing an accelerator on a car. (*The God Catchers,* p. 165)

There is a world of difference between repentance and condemnation. Repentance produces godly sorrow and salvation; condemnation produces death.[3] Repentance leads to something better, purer, and healthier; condemnation or "worldly sorrow" produces ever-descending cycles of depression, guilt, and hopelessness.

I am amazed that so few Christians realize the freedom available in God through the cleansing power of heartfelt repentance. Repentance removes the pressure each day when holy filling is your quest and holy frustration is your address.

Is repentance part of your daily worship before God? Do you view it as a morning shower to cleanse the soul and prepare you for pure service to Him?

Our problem is that most of us have a concept of repentance as "an occasional visit to the village of Repentance." God calls us to a lifestyle of repentance, which is living in the village. (*The God Catchers,* p. 165)

PRAYER

Father, please forgive me for so rarely visiting the village of Repentance. Today is a new day, and I choose to begin by moving my heart into the village of Repentance. I'm frustrated by the dichotomy of my longing for You and my fullness with "me." Please forgive me and cleanse me of my unrighteousness and make me more like You. Above all, Lord, let me dwell in Your presence all the days of my life.

God-Ordained Tension Produces God-Ordained Growth

The chase can take you into some of the most challenging circumstances you will ever experience because worship takes you somewhere that you can't go otherwise. It is what you do in those circumstantial moments of divine frustration that determines whether you remain a God Chaser or you become a God Catcher. The first is good, but the second is better; and the truth is that God will constantly move us from the role of chaser to catcher and then to chaser again. After all, we serve a God who moves (and hides).

THE GOD CATCHERS, P. 167

SCRIPTURE READING:

Psalm 42, where the psalmist shows us how to worship our way out of impossibilities with the determined declaration, "For I shall yet praise Him."

Someone of great experience wrote somewhere that "we all, with unveiled face, beholding as in a mirror the glory of the Lord, are being transformed into the same image from glory to glory, just as by the Spirit of the Lord."[4] It seems this process takes place not so much in a static church pew as in a dynamic journey or the passionate pursuit of Him who is holy.

God expects us to gather as a community for worshiping, caring, and equipping for the "work of the ministry."[5] Yet too many of us strip off our running gear and cease the chase the moment we step out of a worship facility or church meeting. We stop short of God's best when we cut short the growth process I call "chasing God."

Where have you grown the most in your walk with God? Was it always pleasant, peaceful, and stress-free? Was it worth it? Are you prepared to keep on chasing Him, though the chase will take you into even more growth periods marked by obstacles, opposition, and awkwardness?

A developing child may grow by merely eating food, with most of the increase taking the form of body fat. It is better if the child eats healthy food, exercises vigorously, and then gets plenty of rest. The modern church seems to excel at two of the three activities, while virtually ignoring the component of spiritual exercise.

Nothing of importance happens in your spiritual life if you avoid pursuits that require you to stretch and exert yourself far beyond your comfort zone. This is what it means to go from glory to glory. The Christian life isn't a destination (that is, your personal pew at a prime location in the church sanctuary); it is an exciting, ever-changing journey of faith that constantly requires you to become more than you have been in Him.

What do you see most often in the church: "destination-based," single-event spectator Christianity, or "faith-based" pursuit of God and the continuous progression to the next phase of His glory? How would you describe your life in Christ to this point?

God births a frustration in your heart that compels you to pursue Him for more and more of His presence, which in turn makes you want Him even more! This is the only true marriage made in heaven.

> Our faith isn't based on feelings, but it is *fueled by passion*. We anchor our faith on the things God said and promised in His inspired Word, but passion provides the courage and drive to pursue and serve the God of the Word. (*The God Catchers*, p. 166)

Your greatest growth spurts will not come in the moments of His visitation; they will come *later*, in the periods of holy frustration that follow the visitation. He imparts fresh strength to you every time you successfully hurdle the desire to quit the chase or lie down and give up. The moment you look up from "the bottom" to praise Him anyway, He rushes to meet you again. When you make up your mind to lift your hands in praise and wait upon Him, He raises you higher. The process couldn't be any more divine or any more painful. This is the God-ordained life of a God Chaser—and the triumph of a God Catcher.

Think of the testimonies you've heard and read in your life and in the Scriptures. Which testimonies stood out the most to you—the testimonies of divine visitation, or the testimonies of divine visitation at the end of tremendous tests, trials, and difficulties? What God Chaser/God Catcher events in your life will speak louder to your unsaved friends?

We are called into a life of dynamic, real-life faith punctuated by alternate waves of nearly unbearable spiritual hunger and the unspeakable joy of His intimate answer to our hunger. I call this state of God-ordained tension "living at frustration's address on Holy Hunger Street in Divine Desperation" (*The God Catchers,* p. 167).

PRAYER

Father, it is true that my pursuit of You has taken me far beyond my comfort zone into places and situations I would never have gone on my own. Yet I am determined to move beyond the "good" place of a God Chaser into the "best" place of a God Catcher. Grant me the grace and faith to say yes to You even when every cell of my being wants to say no and give up. I'm determined to pursue You with the same passion in bad times as I do in good times. All I know is that I can't seem to get enough of You, but I'm determined to try!

Embrace the Pain
That Attracts His Presence

Pain and brokenness probably brought you to Him in the first place, and pain and brokenness will certainly lead you back to Him without fail. Have you noticed that the thing God runs to is the very thing we run from? "The Lord is near to those who have a broken heart" (and we do everything we can to avoid the pain of brokenness).[6]

THE GOD CATCHERS, P. 170

SCRIPTURE READING:

Psalm 34:17–22, in which David reveals how the weakness of our humanity can attract the infinite strength of divinity.

Moses understood the value of weakness, pain, and brokenness. Early in his miraculous life, his quick temper led him to commit murder in a foolhardy attempt to deliver God's people in his own strength and wisdom.[7]

A lifetime later, we find him leading the children of Israel as a mature spiritual leader with proven leadership skills. Yet Moses revisited his human weakness and yielded to anger once again, striking the rock of divine supply rather than simply speaking as God commanded.[8]

Moses was to use the rod of authority to gather the people together, but he was to use spoken words of petition to model the new covenant relationship between humanity and the Rock of Divinity. When Moses struck the rock, he struck God's representation of the preincarnate Christ and disqualified himself from entering the land of promise. In God's mercy, Moses still obtained a far greater promise when he saw the face of God on the Mount of Transfiguration.[9]

(This man knew a thing or two about the way God works through the weaknesses of men.)

How often does anger or some other human weakness seem to intervene and hinder your chase for God? When it happens, do you try to hide your failure, or do you repent and offer it and your weakness to God as an offering of brokenness?

How do you embrace pain without reveling in the attention it brings you? There is a clear difference between admitting your sin or weakness before God as you seek His face and grace to do better and clinging to your favorite sin or weakness as you seek sympathy from God and man.

The alcoholic who clings to the bottle while crying for mercy receives neither grace nor mercy from either source. It is when he smashes the bottle and displays his bankruptcy to God that he discovers divine mercy and grace flooding his life. The purpose of the "embrace" is to seek the Father's face, not to gain permission and blessing to grovel in past failures or weaknesses permanently. Again, we go from glory to glory, not from offense to offense.

Have you ever tried to cling to a problem just long enough to wring some sympathy out of friends, companions, or God Himself? (Welcome to the human race.) Have you experienced the freedom that comes from truly embracing your pain and offering it to God with your broken heart? What happened?

Pain is pain, but if you can seek Him in the darkness of your midnight, your pain can become the wind beneath your wings that lifts you into His presence!

. . . Brokenness can come through catastrophic sorrow, calamity, or sin. It also can come through our determination to seek Him, obey Him, and dare impossible things at His prompting. That is contrived brokenness and self-imposed humbling. Fasting is one way to do this. (*The God Catchers,* pp. 169–70)

You already know that problems and difficulties come along naturally in life, but have you learned how to humble yourself before Him through

fasting and prayer? Are you willing to embrace your pain to attract His presence?

Paul was a God Chaser who was always looking for the next place God would break out over a city and nation. His compulsive addiction to pursue God and His purposes made him well acquainted with brokenness. (*The God Catchers,* p. 170)

PRAYER

Lord, I'm so hungry for You that I'm willing to embrace the pain of brokenness just to see Your face once more. I'm not eager to experience the heartache of trials in this life, but I will endure it in Your name and seek You while I go through it. I prefer to humble myself daily by denying myself and by taking up my cross to pursue You; but through it all, my goal is to dwell in Your presence and behold Your beauty.

Living in the Tension of Divine Discontent, We Worship Him Every Step of the Way

Paul lived in a constant state of godly tension and divine discontent. He expressed his unwavering hunger for God in the midst of a life littered with constant adversity and impossible obstacles. He repeatedly followed the Lord to the very gates of death and worshiped Him every step of the way.

THE GOD CATCHERS, P. 170

SCRIPTURE READING:

Philippians 4:11–12, where Paul the apostle explains his use of the phrase "being content" with the threefold simultaneous combination of hunger, abundance, and need.

The same man who said he had learned to be content in whatever condition he found himself actually lived perpetually in a condition of divine discontent. The apostle Paul wasn't lying or stretching the truth. He had learned to find holy contentment in the midst of divine discontent.

This is the pattern of a chronic God Chaser. Paul was well practiced in the art of "running his fingers endlessly over the folds of the veil" for the latest place of access to divinity. This man lived with divine discontent.

"Wait a minute. Didn't Paul say he had learned to be content in any state or condition?" you may ask. Yes, he did. He also went on to define what he meant by being "content": "Not that I speak in regard to need, for I have learned in whatever state I am, to be content: I know how to be abased, and I know how to abound.

Everywhere and in all things *I have learned both to be full and to be hungry, both to abound and to suffer need.*"[10] (*The God Catchers,* p. 170)

Divine discontent differs from human discontent in one all-important way: you experience divine discontent because you hunger for more of God; you long to do more and accomplish more in His name according to His purposes.

Human discontent usually centers on the unfulfilled wants and desires of the fleshly trio: me, myself, and I. At best, it focuses on the unfulfilled wants and needs of other people, but not necessarily at the instigation of God. As I stated in *The God Catchers* concerning Paul's life:

This Pharisee-turned-apostle was a chronic God Chaser who constantly reached out for more of God, for more souls, and for more victory over the arrayed forces of darkness. His life was a great search for one more encounter with God and one more opportunity to please and worship the One who died for him. His writings express a rich rhetoric of divine frustration: "Do you not know that those who run in a race all run, but one receives the prize? *Run in such a way that you may obtain it . . . I discipline my body and bring it into subjection,* lest, when I have preached to others, I myself should become disqualified."[11] (p. 171)

Perhaps it isn't wrong to invest your life in satisfying certain kinds of human discontent, but would you rather invest your life in God's best or man's best? Do you prefer the rewards received from pleasing men or the rewards received only through the pursuit of God and His purposes? (The choice truly is yours and yours alone.)

It should be understood that God Chasers fulfill their divine mission in countless ways, including ways not typically seen inside the four walls of a church or meeting hall. Many fulfill their divine call by feeding poor people, caring for sick people, and supplying the needs of the destitute groups across the globe.

Your earthly occupation has little, if anything, to do with your ability to chase God unless you do something clearly unethical or immoral to make a living. Simply pursue Him as your first love until you know what He wants you to do, then do it with all of your might. (Most people who criticize and call "unspiritual" those who meet human needs in Jesus' name rarely venture out of their padded pews to meet any needs but their own.)

God used a Carpenter to redeem the world, a fisherman to preach the first evangelistic message, a table waiter to heal the sick, and a classically trained Jewish rabbi and seminarian to reach the non-Jewish world and write most of the instruction manual for the Christian Church. Their common qualification was their chronic compulsion as God Chasers.[12]

Somehow, I can't picture Paul settling down into a comfortable church pew. He would keep seeing that prize and start "shadowboxing" in the middle of a service and ruin everything. (*The God Catchers,* p. 171)[13]

PRAYER

Father, I refuse to settle down in contentment. I'm too hungry for Your presence and too passionate about Your purposes. I'm helplessly, hopelessly, and eternally hungry for more of Your presence; and the more I get, the more I must have. The more I have, the more I want to give it away to others as I follow You.

When Praise and Worship Pierce the Heavens, God's Sudden Visitation Shakes the Earth

Once we learn how to worship and sing and chase Him even in a dreary midnight hour, we will accomplish more than just having a "sudden visitation" from Him. When God heard the worship rising from that Philippian prison cell, He came so suddenly that His coming triggered an earthquake that shook chains off more than just Paul and Silas. The Bible says that all the prisoners were set free.[14]

THE GOD CATCHERS, PP. 172–73

SCRIPTURE READING:

Acts 16:16–34, where a bloodied pair of evangelists launches the first New Testament prison ministry by leading a rowdy worship service from prisoners' stocks. In the end, they worship God's glory down to earth and introduce their jailer's family to Christ.

Just when it seems safe enough to settle in and relax in the temples of man's making, those troublemakers from heaven blow in through the doors. They are "normal" in every respect except one—they have a strange fixation with the manifest presence of God.

In biblical days, they used to wear camel hair coats and eat strange diets. Some of them even paraded around town naked or called the local ministers snakes (no, I'm not promoting such behavior today).

Today's breed of troublemaker generally remains fully clothed, eats in all of the usual restaurants, and converses politely with local pastors and visiting evange-lists. What you remember most about these troublemakers is that look of hunger in their eyes. You get the strange feeling that they've seen or experienced Something greater than most churches can offer or even claim to possess. They burn with so much passion for God that it is almost embarrassing. For better or for worse, more and more of them are calling themselves "God Chasers."

> God Chasers are so frustrated at times that they make everyone else feel frus-trated too. It seems that whatever they have is "catching." The radical God Chasers who become God Catchers have a way of entering our meetings with their hair still smoking from fresh encounters in an upper room somewhere. They are always looking for another worship fire to fan with their passion, so God tends to show up and make it nearly impossible to conduct church as usual. (*The God Catchers,* p. 171)

How did you catch the God Chaser bug? What or who possessed you to turn your life upside down so you could put His pursuit at the top of your life agenda? How would you describe the God Chasers the Lord sent into your life? How would you describe yourself?

God Chasers have a hard time fitting into the "church as usual" mold. Very often their presence and the passion and single-minded focus they bring to the act of worship seem to reduce "church as usual" to empty acts of religious procedure. Their passionate search for God's face can create a lot of discom-fort for people interested in preserving the status quo at any cost.

There is a clear difference between God Chasers and God Fakers or God Flakes. God Fakers pretend to be spiritual, but they are more interested in the approval and respect of men than in the manifest presence of God. The fastest route to winning that approval most often involves producing a false image of the latest move of God in the earth.

God Flakes are lightweight, dried-out, half-baked imitations of the real thing. They all come out of the same hypocrisy box littered with rewards and gifts attractive to man-pleasers, and they are more interested in attracting the attention of men than the attention of God. Once they win the attention, they do all they can to keep it on themselves.

True God Chasers, on the other hand, attempt to keep their eyes on Him despite the ups and downs that life brings their way. They will do everything in their power to divert all attention, praise, and honor toward God and away from themselves because they know that is a key to turning visitation into habitation.

What are your motives for pursuing God's presence? Do you want to be part of the latest "God thing" in the church, or are you genuinely hungry for God Himself? Do you concern yourself more with the opinions of men or the manifest presence of God?

The significance of living at frustration's address isn't that we are suffering for more of the Lord; it is that we have learned to worship and praise Him regardless of our circumstances or status in life. Our contentment isn't based on what happens to us or what comes our way; it is based solely upon His love for us. It is the essence of a "fasted life" devoted to the pursuit of His face. (*The God Catchers*, p. 172)

Do you reserve your praise and worship for Him solely for the good times of divine visitation, or do you lavish worship upon Him day and night, in good times and bad?

PRAYER

Lord, I don't claim to know much, but I know this much: I need You. I hunger for You. I thirst for You. My soul pants for You. All of the wonders, gifts, attractions, and blessings of humanity cannot equal a mere thirty seconds in Your presence—yet I want more. I thank You for everything You did yesterday and in years gone by; but I want to see what You can do today; and I admit right now that I will want even more tomorrow. I am in passionate pursuit of Your presence, Lord, and nothing less will do.

It's Better to Follow Him Through the Pain Than to Seek Easier Paths for Personal Gain

Something wonderful is coming to the frustrated residents of Holy Hunger Street. The God of More Than Enough is coming in the fullness of time, and some divinely discontented God Chasers are about to "catch" God by His design. Something holy and glorious is about to invade and overwhelm your church, your city, and your home. Can you embrace the frustration required for those who wait on the Deity?

THE GOD CATCHERS, P. 175

SCRIPTURE READING:

Romans 8:35–9:5, where Paul, the apostle of faith and power, describes the assurance we have in Christ and then grieves for his countrymen so deeply that he says, "I have great sorrow and continual grief in my heart."

All of this talk about living in the village of Repentance at frustration's address can be depressing if you fail to see the big picture and understand the goal of it all. Yes, there is method in this madness. Consider some of the great phrases in God's Word: you reap what you sow;[15] those who hunger for righteousness will be filled;[16] love the Lord your God with everything you've got;[17] seek Him while He may be found[18]—the list goes on and on.

All of the central themes of God's Word have one focus expressed in various ways: chase God; hunger for His presence; seek to see His face. The wonderful thing about God, which I can't stress enough, is that He doesn't hide so that He cannot be found. We must remember at all times that He is hiding carefully so that we *can* find Him.

Do you ever feel discouraged and hopeless in your pursuit of His presence? What helped you pick up the pace of the chase once more? Are you able to accept your destiny to continually pursue the God who hides?

Another life-changing truth about God Chasing is that when He comes, He tends to bless everyone in the vicinity of the God Chasers who catch Him. The only Christians in the prison were Paul and Silas the night they started praising God through their pain. When they were finished, God showed up and set everyone free.[19]

When God really shows up and manifests His glory, everyone who experiences it receives an impartation of His nature that leaves him better than when he came. Somehow each person finds himself loving the lost more than ever before. He has such godly compassion for broken and destitute people that he can no longer pass them by without doing something for them in Christ's name.

In your experience, have you seen people grow compassionate and evangelistic toward non-Christians after a genuine God encounter? What happened in your life?

Paul didn't have a problem with "inward focus." His entire life and ministry exploded outward from his first thirty-second encounter with the manifest presence of God on the Damascus Road. He didn't leave that encounter satisfied; he left it eternally and incurably hungry for more of God, along with an unquenchable desire to bring others into His presence—even if it cost him his earthly life!

When was the last time we thought about our "countrymen according to the flesh"? Did we leave our first encounter with God and turn our focus to self or to God and the lost world Jesus came to save? (*The God Catchers,* pp. 173–74)

We all need the big picture of God's purposes to help us navigate the small passages of life's journey and bring His glory to our cities. So how do we cope with today's challenges while drawing strength from our faith in His visitation tomorrow?

Embrace the pregnancy; pull the purposes of God close to you and don't run from the pain that comes with them. Hold the course, and don't abort what God is trying to do in and through you. God is trying to birth something holy in you. Every earthly mother knows that frustration and even desperation are natural components of the healthy birth process. (*The God Catchers*, p. 175)

PRAYER

Father, I refuse to be separated from the holy hunger You've imparted in my life. I would rather follow You through the pain of giving supernatural birth to Your purposes than go my own way in directions free of pain, challenge, or difficulty. In the end I would still be separated from the One I love the most. I'll hold the course and bring Your purposes to full term in my life.

Godly Passion and God's Presence Meet Together in the Church

The church needs to rediscover the power of passion for God. When godly passion is birthed in the church, God's presence enters through the door once again. Jesus said: "Nevertheless I have this against you, that you have left your first love. Remember therefore from where you have fallen; repent and do the first works, or else I will come to you quickly and remove your lampstand from its place—unless you repent."[20]

THE GOD CATCHERS, P. 177

SCRIPTURE READING:

Revelation 2:1–7, in which Jesus warns the church that He holds one thing against it—it left its first love.

For centuries, Christians have read the passage in which God said, "I, the LORD your God, am a jealous God, visiting the iniquity of the fathers on the children to the third and fourth generations of those who hate Me, but showing mercy to thousands, to those who love Me and keep My commandments."[21] It is a good thing to read the Scriptures; our wrong thinking causes problems.

When we read that we serve a jealous God, we think of the characteristics of a jealous man. Jealous men often manifest jealousy because they are immature, insecure, or excessively and wrongly possessive. God matches none of these descriptions.

He is right to say He has exclusive rights to our love and allegiance as our Creator and Redeemer. He is right when He says He is completely righteous and we are completely in the wrong. He is right when He says we must seek Him first as our first love. He is right to say that He loved us first.

What do you think of when you hear someone say, "We serve a jealous God"? As a God Chaser, have you made Him Your first love and first priority in life? How?

We need to learn how to leave a worship service hungrier than when we came. If you want to be a God Catcher, you must learn how to live contentedly with divine desperation and holy hunger at frustration's address!

. . . The process of pursuit begins with "repentance on bended knee," not with religious procedures or proud proclamations of revival. First you enter the "zip code" of God's presence, the realm of repentance and the contrite or humble heart. (*The God Catchers,* pp. 176–77)

With so many individuals and churches today claiming to have an ongoing visitation of God, it is tempting for believers and preachers who want more to resist the formulas, twelve-point plans, and guaranteed keys to igniting revival. Some of the information may be helpful, but shortcuts produce mostly man-made results that fall short of the true potential available through a true visitation and habitation of God.

The manifest presence of the Reviver—and revival, the natural fruit of His presence—comes only to those who learn how to wait upon God and put Him first in true repentance, prayer, praise, and worship.

How do you separate the Real Thing from all the false imitations and false promises of divine visitation? How do you seek visitation and habitation by the one true Reviver of humanity and the church—with revival formulas or through old-fashioned repentance and openly displayed hunger for divinity?

Once repentance prepares you, it is passion that propels you in the chase to catch Him . . .

It takes a determined God Chaser to deliver what God desires and become a God Catcher. (*The God Catchers,* pp. 177–78)

PRAYER

Father, make us so hungry for Your presence that we are miserable, frustrated, and totally obsessed with You. Cause us to long for You so deeply that we make constant "nagging phone calls" to heaven, saying, "Daddy, I want You!" May the pursuit of Your presence become the magnificent obsession of our lives.

Impart to us a massive, life-changing, life-disrupting hunger that makes us desperate for You. Set our hearts on fire with passion.

Father, break out in churches around the world. Invade churches of every type. Break out in bars, in shopping malls, on farms, in schools, at traffic lights, and at football games. We take the limits off You, Lord, because our hunger knows no limits. (*The God Catchers,* p. 178)

Only God Chasers Can Become God Catchers

Would You Climb a Tree of Destiny to Meet Me?

What would you pay to spend just thirty seconds in the manifest presence of God? To what lengths would you go to follow Saul into the Deity's rarefied light for half a minute if it would transform your life and the world as you know it?

How "low" would you stoop to ascend to the heavenlies with God? Would you climb a tree, break an alabaster box, cry out in beggar's robes, or defy the combined will of a legion of demons to call out to Him?

Some will pay nothing and receive the same. Others will invest all they have and more for one moment in the presence of God. The answer depends solely upon the value you place on God's presence.

Learn to Mark Time God's Way

Children don't measure the passage of time the way we do. For a little baby, thirty seconds away from Mommy can seem like eternity. The older we get, the easier it becomes for us to handle separation from our parents—and from God's presence. It just gets harder to recover the "joy of encounter" with Him.

THE GOD CATCHERS, P. 181

SCRIPTURE READING:

John 3:30; Philippians 3:13–14, in which a prophet and an apostle show us how to tell time and mark our spiritual progress.

As the father of three beautiful daughters, I consider myself one of the most blessed men on the planet. Yet I dread the very day most anticipated by each of my daughters. Each one of them dreams of the day her daddy gives her away in marriage, but there is a part of Daddy that doesn't want to give away any of them.

If I live to be 120 years old, those girls will always be my babies, and I'll never get enough of warm embraces and happy faces. I have the feeling that our heavenly Father feels the same frustration about our so-called growing-up process. If I understand the biblical view on this subject, we are to grow wiser and more mature in our understanding of God's workings with men while remaining totally childlike in our relationship with Him.

Do you get the feeling that some people want to hurry up and grow up so they can move out of God's house and live on their own? How do you see it? Does the heavenly Father really enjoy His intimate

230

moments with you and others like you? Are you becoming more like a child in His presence or more like an independent adult who feels able to function freely apart from His nearness without a feeling of loss or emptiness?

Have you ever walked into an old family home to look for growth notes on the door frames? They are more common than you might believe. Long before the days of colorful preprinted growth charts, parents used to call their children in on a monthly or yearly basis to stand by a closet door frame. With pencil in hand, they would carefully look across the top of each child's head to mark the height in feet and inches on the frame and place the name and the date beside each mark.

It was only natural for each child to stretch upward toward the highest mark he could reach to proudly demonstrate to Mom and Dad just how much he'd grown since the last measuring. As the years went by, the marks on the door frame crept upward past the door latch to the four-foot mark, then to four and a half feet, five feet, and beyond. Observant visitors can see an entire family growth history displayed on a single door frame if they look for it.

I read somewhere that the apostle Paul also kept track of his progress with a mark: "Brethren, I count not myself to have apprehended: but this one thing I do, forgetting those things which are behind, and reaching forth unto those things which are before, I press toward the mark for the prize of the high calling of God in Christ Jesus."[1]

Are you pressing toward a mark to demonstrate your maturity for the benefit of men, or do you press upward for the mark of a higher call by drawing closer to the Father and by embracing His purposes?

I've learned something in the last few years about the spiritual growth measurement. As I said in *The God Catchers,* "God Chasers become God Catchers when they begin to measure time in terms of absences from His manifest presence" (p. 180).

When you play hide-and-seek with a toddler, you could hide in the same place every time and still see the same incredible joy spread over his face when he finds you in your "hiding place." My daughters used to act as if they hadn't seen me in two weeks, even though I'd been hiding only two minutes. Why? Children do not measure time by the ticks of a clock or the forward progress of clock hands or dials. They measure time in terms of absences: "How long has it been since I held my mommy?" (*The God Catchers*, p. 181)

The object of maturity is to become productive, dependable, and equipped to pass on the family heritage to the new generations that will follow. The object of God Chasing—and our eternal relationship with God—is to become more dependent upon His grace and more addicted to His presence. Perhaps John the Baptist best described the Christian's proper life goal when he told his disciples, "He must increase, but I must decrease."[2] This apparent dichotomy of purpose isn't new to God's kingdom. His Word also commands us to be "wise as serpents and harmless as doves."[3]

How are you managing the dual growth process of the Christian life? Are you growing in Christian maturity for the work of the ministry while becoming more childlike with each God encounter? Have you noticed that some of the greatest leaders in the church exhibit a childlike quality when they speak of Him? (*Wouldn't it be nice if they all did?*)

The moment He comes, the instant the Object of our worship comes, we latch on to His glory and press into His presence. We forget to say "bye" to the day's routines, and we often abandon our friendships and break our conversations mid-sentence to exclaim in breathless joy, "It's Him!" (*The God Catchers*, p. 183)

PRAYER

Father, no matter how mature I become in Your grace, keep me childlike and tender before Your face. I have far to go in the maturity race, but my first priority is to increase my pace to see Your face once more. All I know is that I need You, I want You, and I am compelled to pursue Your presence with all of the passion in my soul. I just want You, Daddy.

Stand on His Promises and Leap into His Arms

Where do you go when there is nowhere else to go? You hang your toes over the edges of God's promises, and "stand still and see." You may have to worship at "midnight" while you embrace your pain, but the fragrance of your brokenness will draw Him close. I can't tell you that everything is going to be all right because God will not force His will upon the will of men or women. But I can tell you that if you break the alabaster box, He will come to you.

THE GOD CATCHERS, PP. 183–84

SCRIPTURE READING:

Romans 8:14–19, where the Bible reveals our status as adopted children of God with the gift of privileged intimacy reserved only for His children.

Some of my most memorable moments in God's presence came in the twilight hours of my strength and ability. They were times of great stress and uncertainty, and seasons of unbearable pain or concern for loved ones who are dear to me. In dire need of help but at the end of my resources and personal endurance, I cried out to Him in absolute surrender and total weakness. Then He came.

I didn't need a written guarantee that every detail would work out according to my wishes because my heavenly Father was there. As long as He was near, I *knew* everything of eternal importance would work out according to His plan. We must learn how to live and stand our ground according to His promises, but once He shows up and embraces us in His grace, faith becomes

233

effortless because His promises become more real and concrete than ever before when we look into His face.

You know you must go through certain trials solely on the basis of God's written promises and your personal knowledge of His faithfulness. However, have you ever reached the end of your strength and cried out to Him in your weakness? Did He come in answer to your brokenness?

There is one thing that will cause God to abandon the worship of the archangels in heaven—it is that desperate cry from the "backyard" called earth. Once He hears that cry, once He hears the crash and tinkle of breaking alabaster boxes and the passionate cries of broken hearts, He comes faster than time itself. He won't leave His heavenly throne for just any nonchalant prayer or sound of casual praise. He comes to those whose divine desperation and holy hunger drive them to cry out in childlike frustration, "I'm going to die if I don't have You!" How hungry are you? (*The God Catchers,* p. 184)

Maturity helps you walk by faith and not by sight during the dry seasons when His visitation is rare and the going is tough. The childlike part of your being, however, brings the balance that keeps you from placing more value on the promises than on the Promiser.

Live and stand by God's Word, but remember that Jesus came to bridge the gap between the Creator and the created, to restore the breach between the heavenly Father and His prodigal children. I read somewhere that He said, "I will be a Father to you, and you shall be My sons and daughters."[4]

Do you wrestle with this balance between the confident walk of faith according to God's Word and the path of total dependence and surrender? Are you able to hold tight to both elements of your high calling?

This is the problem: we have an inborn tendency to use God's Word to grow *independent* from His presence. God's chief delight in the Garden of Eden was the *relationship* He enjoyed with Adam and Eve. He wants that back.

Everything He has done and is doing is designed to restore us to the intimacy of His presence. He gave us His Word as a tool to serve Him victoriously in this life and as a road map to guide us back into His presence. He *never* intended for us to use His Word as a vehicle to distance us from His embrace, to lessen our childlike dependence upon His grace, or to dull our hunger for His presence. (That is the mistake the Pharisees made when they put more emphasis on the letter of the law than on the Spirit of the law.)[5]

The balance comes when your maturity tells you to "hang your toes over the edges of God's promises" and stand by faith while your childlike heart cries out to God as an offering of brokenness and repentance that He cannot refuse. We stand on His promises so that we can leap into His arms.

Have you lost your balance between faith and dependence at times? Are you determined to stand on God's promises through long nights of adversity, even if He doesn't allow you to catch Him today or tomorrow? Are you prepared to praise and worship Him anyway in childlike brokenness and dependence? (Then you know He will come.)

PRAYER

Father, I thank You for the gift of life, but I thank You even more for the gifts of Your presence and Your Word as I walk through this life. Help me grow in faith even as my hunger for Your presence grows greater each day. I will stand on Your promises by faith until the next time I can leap into Your arms and see Your face.

Turn Up the Heat of Your Passion for God Until Your Entire City Catches on Fire!

I pray that someone starts "adjusting the thermostat" in cities around the world. May these desperate "firebrands" turn the dial of passion as high as it will go, saying, "I don't care. I'm not going to stop until the whole city is on fire!" That happens only when people have had a "suddenly," a God-encounter in the temple or an upper room. It happens when people have "waited" on Him long enough to catch their "hair on fire" and have their tongues touched by the fire of God.

THE GOD CATCHERS, PP. 185–86

SCRIPTURE READING:

Acts 2, where true events seem stranger than fiction, and we are reminded how far we have strayed from the fire and might of divine visitation and passionate demonstration of God's power.

Every time I turn to the book of Acts, I remind myself that I am not reading a fairy tale, a morality lesson, a parable, or a work of Christian fiction. The Acts are facts about the force of divine truth as it impacted an entire nation and the world through the lives of a few very ordinary people barely two thousand years ago.

Even a casual reading of the events on that particular day of pentecost boggles the mind with the scope of God's power to intervene in man's affairs with a little bit of fire.

It all began with an extended prayer meeting where 120 or so people were engulfed by a loud, Spirit-driven wind feeding a visible fire from heaven that set their hair on fire. Evidently the sound of His sudden coming was so loud that it drew a crowd of multiplied thousands.[6]

How comfortable are you with the words *power, engulfed,* and *fire*? These words describe the birth or infantile beginning of the church. Are they still part of your life or the life of the church today, now that we have "come so far"?

The people in Jerusalem were shocked to see 120 country folks (most of them from the county of Galilee) stagger downstairs like a gang of drunks to weave down the street with their hair still smoking and their lips speaking the languages of virtually every race, nationality, or ethnic group represented there.[7]

To top it all off, a rash fisherman who had recently lost his nerve in front of scores of high-level witnesses suddenly began to preach to the masses with such power that three thousand people answered his altar call![8]

I'm reminded that our chief purpose in this life is to become the kindling of God, the fuel of the Divine Fire, the flammable material in the Deity's hand. God always signals His extended visitations with fire.

Make sure you come before Him dry, thirsty, and hungry. Your job is to become the fuel of God. Fire without fuel is a smoldering failure waiting to happen, a brief and bright disappointment on the horizon of human hope.

Approach His presence with a burning desire for ignition. I've been told that when John Wesley was asked about the "secret" to his powerful ministry, he said, "I just set myself on fire for God and people come to see me burn." (*The God Catchers*, pp. 184–85)

The phrases "kindling of God" and "flammable material in the Deity's hand" may prompt uncomfortable images of heat and death. As a God Chaser, are you prepared to become the fuel of the consuming God you pursue? Is the heat of your passion high enough to ignite your life and sustain a flame so bright that it can be seen by the people around you?

If someone asked you to choose one word that most accurately describes the modern church, I don't think *passion* would be your word of choice. Another *p* word comes to mind, and it isn't very flattering or satisfying: it is the word *passive*. As I mentioned in *The God Catchers,*

> I'm tired of the church being a spiritual thermometer that simply reflects the ambient temperature of society. A thermostat isn't made to merely reflect or measure ambient temperature. It is made to predict and control its surroundings. (p. 185)

The gap between a thermometer and a thermostat is so wide that it takes a supernatural transformation to complete the changeover in a church. The good news is that the process takes place in one heart at a time. In other words, if you allow *your* passion for His presence to draw Him near, He may ignite your heart and use you to raise the ambient temperature of the hearts around you.

> A supernatural thermostat, a zealot for the kingdom, says, "I'm going to keep throwing myself on the fire until my passion for His presence draws Him to this place." That is what you and I are supposed to do in our cities and nation. "I know what it looks like out there, but I'm not moved by that. I'm raising the thermostat to move it to the level it is supposed to be." (*The God Catchers*, p. 185)

Are you ready to throw yourself on the Divine Fire until His presence comes near? Are you discouraged by the passivity and apathy around you? What are you prepared to do about it? Will you do what it takes to "raise the thermostat" in your church and city?

PRAYER

Father, I was born to burn for You. Give me the courage and strength to press through every obstacle with my passion for Your presence. I'm determined to fan the flames of my passion until You engulf the church with the fire of Your presence once more. Then we will ignite our passion for You until our city catches the fire and bows its knee in Your presence.

Learn to Stay in a Tender Stage of Brokenness

God doesn't come to you simply because problems come along; He comes because you are tender. If you can learn to stay at that tender stage of brokenness without the necessity of contrary circumstances, then you will be "falling on the Rock" as opposed to having "the Rock fall on you."[9] *Both create the same fragrance of brokenness, but one is self-induced and the other one is circumstantially induced.*

THE GOD CATCHERS, P. 187

SCRIPTURE READING:

1 Peter 2:7–8; 1 Corinthians 1:26–29; 2 Corinthians 12:9–10, in which we read descriptions of the foundation of human weakness leaning on divine strength upon which God is building His kingdom.

Paul the apostle, the man most Christians rank just below Christ on the spiritual power scale, said something in one of his letters that seems very odd. He wrote, "When I am weak, then I am strong."[10] This mighty apostle knew the power God releases to us when we offer Him the brokenness and limitations of our lives. Paul went beyond his personal experience to *define our calling* with what I call the "roll call of the weak":

For you see your calling, brethren, that not many wise according to the flesh, not many mighty, not many noble, are called. But God has chosen the foolish things of the world to put to shame the wise, and God has chosen the weak things of the world to put to shame the things which are mighty; and the base things of

239

the world and the things which are despised God has chosen, and the things which are not, to bring to nothing the things that are, that no flesh should glory in His presence.[11]

It seems that God has eliminated every hint of human pride in the divine equation of His perfect will. Pride shows up when we try to reinsert it where it doesn't belong. In place of our pride, He gave us the privilege of leaning on Him for divine strength, wisdom, righteousness, love, and grace as His children.

Do you approach your life in Christ by leaning totally upon the strength and presence of God, or by making brief and casual connection in the Spirit through the slightest contact with the Deity? Which approach most closely imitates the pattern of approach modeled by Jesus Christ, Paul, Peter, John, and Mary, the sister of Martha?

I've learned that if you want to attract His presence, brokenness is His favorite perfume and tears are His favorite anointing. When something happens in the course of life that breaks your heart or bruises your soul, pull the pain to you and offer it to the Lord. There have been times when I felt that I couldn't hurt anymore and live, but suddenly I sensed Him there.

It dawned on me that when that brokenness occurs in my life, He shows up and says, "Oh, I see you've put on My favorite fragrance again." He doesn't revel in our pain or loss, but He does respond to the brokenness and need in our lives. (*The God Catchers,* p. 186)

I'm determined to remain in a state of tender brokenness before God because I am absolutely addicted to His presence. I've had a foretaste of eternity's bliss, and I discovered that the Father longs to reveal Himself to us now as well as then. If the fragrance of brokenness attracts the Love of my soul, then I will have brokenness as my constant companion.

If I have a choice between the self-induced brokenness created by my passionate hunger and the bitter brokenness produced by contrary circumstances, my first choice is obvious. Both will come my way, but I want His presence near me as much as possible. My life has become a continual quest to string together as many divine encounters as I can.

Does all this talk of brokenness and God addiction raise the price of His presence too high for comfort? It is just as accurate to speak of running to Daddy at every opportunity, whether the emergency involves a genuine injury or situation, or a contrived opportunity to sit on His knee once again. The price is still too high for human payment, but are you willing to pursue Him at any cost in the hope that He will turn and allow Himself to be caught in your passionate longing?

All I can say is that I have been "smitten of Him," and I hope that I'm so contagious that you catch the same disease. I'm out to make you and those around you "carriers" of the disease of spiritual *dis*-ease and divine desperation. My hope is that in some way I can leave some trail signs or erect a few landmarks to help you find your own way into His presence. (*The God Catchers,* p. 186)

PRAYER

Father, it is difficult to describe my hunger for You, so I must revert to the words of my childhood to tell You how I feel. Daddy, I want You! I'm not fast enough to catch You and I'm not strong enough to hold You—but I'm weak enough to need You and lean on You with all of my being. Please accept my offering of brokenness and urgent longing. You are my Hope and my Salvation, my Chief Joy and the object of my passionate pursuit.

THE FIFTH DAY

When We Feed God with Our Hunger, He Satisfies Us with Living Water

When Jesus met the Samaritan woman at the well that day, He had a divine appointment at the well of life. A thirsty soul was waiting for a miracle. The twelve professional preachers who followed Jesus returned to the well from the local café and wondered why He didn't want any of the natural food or drink they brought Him. He had been fed by the hunger of the woman at the well, and He satisfied her thirst with living water from the heart of God.

THE GOD CATCHERS, PP. 187–88

SCRIPTURE READING:

John 4:1–34, where Jesus satisfies a desperate woman's thirst for God with living water from the river of God.

For some reason known only to God, He chose to reveal certain divine patterns in His relationship with humanity. It seems clear that God doesn't meet needs indiscriminately. He takes great care to invest more of His infinite supply in hungry, thirsty, and desperate souls than in casual criers and apathetic worshipers. (The pattern doesn't seem to vary according to outward appearances. He shows no partiality to the color of human skin, gender, or even our outward religious trappings and credentials.)

By the accepted religious standards of the day, Jesus shouldn't have even talked to the Samaritan woman. Even the most moral of Jewish teachers would have no problem calling a Samaritan a dog in public places. By man's religious standards, the woman's earthly circumstances disqualified her from any contact with a holy God. They forgot that God's standards aren't based on human morality or good deeds; they are based on humanity's thirst for the Deity's fullness. When God saw a thirsty soul in need of a miracle, He issued a divine assignment, and Divinity intercepted humanity at Jacob's well.[12]

What does God see when He looks over the ramparts of heaven and into your soul? Does He see a heart filled with the fullness of the world of men, or a heart hungry and thirsty for more of the Bread of heaven and the Water of Life? Are there emptiness and passionate longing in you that might attract the fullness in Him?

Difficult circumstances create brokenness, and He runs to our brokenness. Why do we run from what He runs to? Point all the pain produced by unfulfilled broken dreams toward Him. Allow the presence of God to open up new windows for you.

We can never have what we need to have until we can get hungrier than we've been because our capacity for being filled is totally determined by the capacity of our emptiness. We must learn to leave services hungrier than when we came.

The people who seem the hungriest are the same people who know how to *worship Him* in spirit and in truth. They have learned to hunger and thirst for the same One they worship and adore. (*The God Catchers*, p. 187)

Many of us must overcome a mental hurdle before we can accept the idea of becoming a God Chaser. We were taught that once we received Christ as Lord and Savior, then our part was over. After all, we *are* saved by grace and not by works. Fortunately God graciously leads us back to His Word to see how He reacted to passionate people such as Peter, Paul, Mary of Magdalene, and Mary of Bethany. We notice that even Paul, the apostle of faith, talked about pressing for the mark, and the light begins to dawn. Faith and grace save us, but passionate pursuit becomes our first and greatest calling from that point on!

Will you be a Mary, a passionate box-breaker bearing the fragrance of brokenness? First, you must abandon the crowd of voices trying to steal or withhold worship from God in the name of preserving man's program. Mary was interested in His presence. She was just glad He was there.

Everyone else wanted to see what he could *get* or gain from Him, but she wanted to see what she could *give* to Him. Church is not what you get out of it; church is what you give to Him. (*The God Catchers,* p. 188)

By now, this concept of giving to God instead of merely seeking to get something from Him is no longer new. But have you taken it beyond the status of a concept to the status of a lifestyle?

The Father is bending over the ramparts of heaven. He hears the irresistible crackle and the tinkle of breaking alabaster boxes. *Is that the sound of your heart breaking?* An incredible fragrance is filling the atmosphere, and I hear the rumors of His sudden approach.

Can you hear the footsteps of Jesus coming as He says, "I smell My favorite fragrance"? He is near to them who are of a broken heart; He can't turn His face away from brokenness. (*The God Catchers,* pp. 188–89, italics mine)

PRAYER

Father, it's me again. Sorry, but I can't seem to get enough of You. I've done it again. I broke the box of my passionate longing and brokenness right in front of You. I know You can't turn Your face away from my brokenness, but then I can't bear to turn my face away from You either! I know it's Your favorite perfume, but there's more where this came from. I'm gathering it in my heart even now in anticipation of the next time we meet. Daddy, I need You!

I Will Not Offer Him a Sacrifice That Does Not Cost Me Personal Sacrifice

Mary sacrificed her future for His present presence. What would you give to be saturated in His presence for just thirty seconds? It's time to break your alabaster box.

If it doesn't cost you anything, then it's someone else's brokenness. Worship that costs you nothing is momentary, but worship that costs you goes with you.

THE GOD CATCHERS, P. 190

SCRIPTURE READING:

2 Samuel 24:23–24, where David reveals the importance of value and personal cost in our gifts to God. He is more interested in their "heart value" than in their monetary value.

One of the statements floating around in church circles claims that "20 percent of the church does all of the work to meet the needs of the other 80 percent." Whether it is based on solid research, I can't say. Yet I'm convinced it is true anyway. I bring it up because this statement mirrors a similar problem with corporate *worship* in the church. As I noted in *The God Catchers*:

Often the presence of God hangs heavy in our prayer rooms and churches, but ten minutes after we leave them, the presence has lifted from us. Are you frustrated with that process?

The secret may be that the fragrance that drew His presence didn't come from you. Were you enjoying the fragrance of someone else's brokenness? Perhaps that is why you have nothing to carry home with you once you leave a service.

If you're just enjoying the fragrance of others, you may never know whose brokenness brings fragrance in the room. I can tell you this: God's manifest presence will go home only with the one whose brokenness summoned Him. (p. 189)

Have you felt the frustration that comes when God's presence lifts just moments after a worship gathering ends? Let me repeat the question: "Were you enjoying the fragrance of someone else's brokenness?"

Too many Christians float through life without any serious commitment to God and His kingdom. They accept Christ to get their ticket to heaven and simply hitchhike their way through the rest of their earthly existence. They let the tithes and offerings of others carry the weight of evangelism and ministry to the local flock. They allow the labors of others to carry the ministry of Christ to their children, to the poor, to the hungry, and to those in need of personal support in life.

Even the act of worship is too taxing for Christian hitchhikers. They are content to ride on the prayers, praise, and worship of others without ever seeking God's face for themselves. Oddly enough, they are often the first to complain or question God about why His presence lifts so fast once the real worshipers leave a meeting. "This couldn't be *real revival,*" they say. "The *pastor* must have done something to make God mad." No, the worshipers who brought God to the party left, and God went home with them.

Most of us have played the part of spiritual hitchhikers sometime in our lives. Have you had your hitchhiking thumb up during worship services recently? Isn't it time to invest the best thing you have to possess the best God has to offer?

When Mary went home the night after she broke her alabaster box of brokenness over Jesus, she still smelled like Him. When she lay down to sleep, she still smelled like Him. When she got up the next morning, she still smelled like Him. (*The God Catchers,* p. 189)

Mary invested all that she had for one encounter with Jesus. She embodied the passion that drives God Chasers around the world. We all want to see Him, sense His presence, and draw near in worship and adoration. The more of Him we get, the more of Him we must have. We find ourselves unable to find satisfaction in passionless church protocols. There is a fire in our bones that launches us in a desperate search for His manifest presence.

Are you a hopeless addict of God's presence, a chronic God Chaser with nothing better to do than follow hard after God? Did God ignite a fire of passion and desire in your heart that made you unfit for any purpose but His own?

Are you desperate for the kind of God encounter that goes with you? This is the key: you must break your own alabaster box. He won't break it for you; you must break it. (*The God Catchers*, pp. 189–90)

PRAYER

Father, I confess my passion has outgrown my ability to contain it once again. I can't help myself, but my heart is broken and I can't get up without Your help. When You gave me a taste of Your goodness, You ruined me for everything less than Your perfection. I'm thankful for every wonderful thing You've made, and I'm thankful for the church and all of Your faithful deeds. But I'm desperate to see and experience all that You can do. Daddy, it's true—I need You.

Only God Chasers Can Become God Catchers

Remember, a baby's cry of weakness can access the strength of the Father faster than the speed of light. If you never chase Him, you can never catch Him. Besides, your weakness will qualify you for a miracle if you put your hunger and desperation on open display. Put a voice to your frustration and cry out to Him.

THE GOD CATCHERS, P. 190

SCRIPTURE READING:

Matthew 4:18–22; Mark 2:14–17; 11:52; where Jesus calls four fishermen—Peter, Andrew, James, John—and a lowly tax collector named Levi to become God Chaser disciples. He also called seven others and challenged the Twelve to an unprecedented three-year pursuit of divinity (with remarkable times of "catching" and being caught) that would change our world forever. A blind man also managed to join the chase whose name will be remembered forever.

Some of us just can't seem to overcome the painful childhood memories of rejection we suffered due to human *favoritism*. We automatically assume that God has favorites just as we do. He doesn't. Four times we are told in the New Testament that God does not show partiality (or "respect of persons").[13] Two times God clearly tells us *not* to show favoritism because it is sin.[14]

The truth is that the things God really favors make it impossible for you to fail as a God Chaser! He isn't interested in your strengths, abilities, accomplishments, or brilliance. He wants you in all of your humanity, complete with your blemishes, weaknesses, faults, and foolishness.

Do you really believe that your weakness will qualify you for a miracle, or did you fall for the old lie that God blesses only the more perfect and well-endowed members of our race? He is more interested in your hunger and desperation than in your innate fullness and wonderful abilities. Which set of gifts will you offer Him?

Bartimaeus is another God Chaser who joined the discipleship chase, yet religion has reduced this very real person to a mythological figure rooted in unreal events. He really existed, and his cries of desperation really did stop God in His tracks! By all religious and cultural standards, Bartimaeus had no business interrupting the Jesus parade at Jericho's gate that day, but hunger wouldn't be denied.

A divine appointment was afoot, but it took a desperate cry of humanity to tap the wellsprings of the Divinity's mercy that day. Casual comments on the efficacy of prayer, the omniscience of God, and the beauty of the Psalms were of no use that day. (They don't do much for us today either.)

It isn't the content of such comments that nullifies their power; it is their lack of passion for God's presence that classifies them as tokens of a religious system "having a form of godliness but denying its power."[15]

Are you desperate for God? It's time to abandon everything that would keep you blind and downtrodden in the dust of your spiritual poverty. Throw off the cloak of man's judgments and religious opinions. Follow the path of blind Bartimaeus. Stand up and let the stench of a life spent begging for the support and approval of man fall away forever. (*The God Catchers,* p. 191)

How many years have you wasted seeking the support and approval of men? How long have you survived on scraps while sitting under the cloak of man's unkind judgments and unwise religious opinions? Are you ready for a change? Are you prepared to follow a

blind man into the light of God's presence? Will you cry out with the passionate desperation of Bartimaeus, no matter how many voices rise up to silence you?[16]

Earthly brokenness creates heavenly openness. When the fountains of the great deep are broken up, the windows of heaven are opened up: "On that day all the fountains of the great deep were broken up, and the windows of heaven were opened." It's as if I can hear the creaking of the heavenly windows beginning to open. It's time to release the cry God can't deny: "Daddy, I want You!" (*The God Catchers,* p. 191)

PRAYER

Father, I can't hold back any longer. I refuse to let even one more divine opportunity pass me by. I'm desperate for You! Nothing less will do; I have to have You. I'm dropping every desire for the approval of men. All I want is to see Your face and to feel Your embrace.

If Bartimaeus could do it, then I can too. I'm in passionate pursuit of Your presence. I'm not big enough, fast enough, or important enough to stop You, Lord, but perhaps my passionate cries can capture Your heart. Jesus, Son of David, have mercy on me! Abba, Daddy, I need You!

Notes

Notes for the Chase

1. See 1 Timothy 2:4. Please understand that this is God's *desire*, but by His design, it is up to each individual person to accept or reject Jesus Christ as Lord and Savior.

2. John 3:30.

3. See Isaiah 55:6.

Week One

1. Tommy Tenney, *The God Chasers* (Shippensburg, PA: Destiny Image Publishers, 1998), p. 2.

2. C. S. Lewis, *The Problem of Pain* (New York: Macmillan, 1977), p. 147.

3. See 2 Corinthians 5:7.

4. See 2 Samuel 7:18.

5. See Hebrews 12:2.

6. See 1 John 4:19.

7. See John 4:23.

8. Tommy Tenney, *The God Catchers* (Nashville: Thomas Nelson, 2000), adapted from a passage on p. 8.

9. Ibid., p. 11.

10. Ibid.

11. Ibid., pp. 11–12.

12. Ibid., p. 12.

Week Two

1. Isaiah 6:5.

2. *The God Catchers,* selected phrases drawn from p. 14.

3. See Daniel 3.

4. *The God Chasers,* p. 16.

5. Ibid.

6. Ibid.

7. Tenney, *The God Chasers*, pp. 139, 149, respectively.

8. *The God Catchers,* p. 20.

9. *The Amplified Bible* (Grand Rapids, MI: Zondervan and the Lockman Foundation, 1987), p. 1402; citing Alexander Souter, *Pocket Lexicon of the Greek New Testament* (London: Oxford University Press, 1916).

10. According to Paul in Galatians 4:6–7, it is entirely appropriate for blood-bought children of God to cry out to God using the familiar term *Daddy*. It should never be used to dismiss or minimize His sovereignty, holiness, or absolutely righteous nature; but it is a unique aspect of the relationship Jesus purchased for us on the cross.

11. *Merriam-Webster's Collegiate Dictionary*, 10th ed. (Springfield, MA: Merriam-Webster, 1994), p. 803.

12. Matthew 22:37, printed emphasis mine, spiritual emphasis the Lord's.

13. Philippians 2:13.

14. *The God Catchers*, adapted from text on p. 30.

15. Ibid., from the closing prayer for Chapter 2, "Burning Lips and Hot Hearts."

Week Three

1. Revelation 3:17.

2. Revelation 3:16.

3. See Matthew 18:6; Mark 9:42; Luke 17:2.

4. See Acts 2:17–18; Titus 2:1–8; 1 John 2:12–14.

5. We read in James 4:17: "Therefore, to him who knows to do good and does not do it, to him it is sin."

6. 1 Peter 1:8.

7. See Acts 3:19 for a balanced picture of godly repentance leading to God-breathed refreshment.

8. See Matthew 5:6, 10; 6:33; Romans 14:17–18.

9. See Isaiah 64:8; Jeremiah 18:6. The passage in Jeremiah specifically refers to Israel, but the warning and the facts of God's metaphor apply equally well to His greater kingdom under the new covenant of Christ.

10. 2 Timothy 3:12.

11. Romans 8:28.

12. Isaiah 53:6.

13. 2 Corinthians 12:9.

14. See Matthew 5:3–10; 23:11–13; Luke 4:18 for selected examples.

15. See John 4:23.

16. See Psalm 27:4.

17. See Luke 10:21; 19:41; John 2:2–7; 11:35.

18. See Psalm 22:3.

19. See 2 Samuel 7:5–13.

20. See 1 Kings 8:27–29.

21. Amos 9:11; see also Acts 15:16.

22. Tommy Tenney, *God's Favorite House* (Shippensburg, PA: Fresh Bread, an imprint of Destiny Image Publishers, 1999), p. 134.

23. Ibid., pp. 7–8, where David's heart for worship is discussed in detail. See also 2 Samuel 6:14–15, 21–22.

24. Prayer reproduced from *The God Catchers*, p. 43.

Week Four

1. See Matthew 10:38–39; 16:24; Mark 8:34; 10:21; Luke 9:23.

2. See Luke 9:62.

3. See Romans 1:17; 2 Corinthians 5:7; Galatians 2:20; 3:11; Hebrews 10:38.

4. See Ephesians 4:11–12.

5. See the "greatest commandment" in Matthew 22:37–40. Although rooted in the Old Testament, this passage remains the best summary of our duty before God in all of the Scriptures. The only difference is that now, through the resurrected Christ, God dwells within us and empowers us to fulfill these commands by His Spirit.

6. See Acts 1:8; Matthew 28:19.

7. See 2 Corinthians 13:5.

8. Our goal must be to honor the God of the church by restoring to biblical patterns the worship and service we offer to Him, while being careful not to ridicule or belittle the church in the process.

9. See Philippians 3:4–14.

10. John 12:21.

11. *The God Catchers*, p. 51.

12. See 1 Chronicles 29:15; Hebrews 11:13; 1 Peter 2:11.

13. See Matthew 5:14–16; Philippians 2:15.

14. Tenney, *The God Chasers*, see the original narrative in Chapter 8: "The Purpose of His Presence," p. 120.

15. Tenney, *God's Favorite House*, Chapter 5: "Turning on the Light of His Glory," p. 71.

Week Five

1. Revelation 3:16.

2. See Matthew 18:6–14; Mark 9:42; Luke 17:2.

3. Revelation 3:17.

4. See Proverbs 29:5.

5. See Isaiah 46:9–10.

6. James Strong, *Strong's Exhaustive Concordance of the Bible* (Peabody, MA: Hendrickson Publishers, n.d.), declare (Hebrew, #5046).

7. See Isaiah 55:8–9.

8. See Philippians 2:8.

9. Luke 9:23.

10. Isaiah 55:6.

11. See Matthew 12:46–50.

12. Mark 10:47.

13. See 1 John 4:19.

14. See Mark 10:47.
15. See Matthew 9:20–22.
16. See Matthew 15:20–28.
17. See Mark 5:1–20.
18. See Mark 2:1–12.

Week Six

1. *The God Catchers,* p. 79.
2. Ibid., p. 81.
3. See 2 Samuel 5:4.
4. See Leviticus 10:1–2.
5. A. B. Bruce, *The Training of the Twelve* (Grand Rapids, MI: Kregel, 1971), p. 541.
6. See Luke 17:12–19.
7. See 1 Corinthians 12:7–12, where Paul described the nine *charis* or grace gifts of the Holy Spirit.
8. See Ephesians 4:8–13, where Paul listed and described the *doma* gifts (often called the leadership gifts or fivefold ministry gifts) for the equipping and training of the saints for the work of the ministry and for the edification (building up) of the body of Christ.
9. *The God Catchers,* p. 91.
10. See Luke 18:2–8.
11. Luke 18:1.
12. *The God Catchers,* p. 94.

Week Seven

1. Judges 2:18; Psalm 101:5.
2. See Kings 4:3.
3. James 5:11 KJV.
4. Hebrews 7:25.
5. See Matthew 9:36; 14:14; 15:32; 20:34; Mark 1:41; 6:34; 8:2; Luke 7:13; 19:41; John 11:35. See also 1 Peter 3:8 and Jude 22.
6. For more on the subject, see Tenney, *God's Favorite House,* pp. 38–39.
7. See Amos 9:13.
8. *The God Catchers,* p. 105.
9. See Joshua 10:12–14, where God made the sun and moon stand still at Joshua's request during a battle for the occupation of the promised land.
10. Jesus resurrected the son of the widow of Nain in Luke 7:11–16, and God delivered Queen Esther, Mordecai, and the Jewish people from wicked Haman in Esther 4:1–3; 6:7–10; and 7:9, respectively.
11. *The God Catchers,* p. 107; verse cited is Matthew 5:6 (italics mine).
12. Ibid., p. 108.
13. Matthew 18:20.
14. Luke 9:23.
15. *Strong's Concordance,* deny (Greek, #533, #720, #4483).

Week Eight

1. See 2 Corinthians 3:18.
2. See 2 Corinthians 3:18.
3. See Mark 10:45; Luke 14:12–14; 1 John 3:16.
4. Matthew 28:19–20.
5. See James 2:19. Even demons understand the basic theology of God's omnipotence. They "believe in God," but obviously that doesn't mean they "know" Him.
6. See Matthew 26:6–13; Mark 14:3–9.
7. 2 Corinthians 4:6–7.
8. See Numbers 14:21.
9. I deal with the concept of "the bread of His presence" versus "stale crumbs of past visitations" in much greater detail in *The God Chasers*, pp. 22–30.
10. Matthew 16:16.
11. Matthew 16:23 (italics mine).
12. Psalm 27:4.
13. See Ephesians 6:10–18.
14. See Philippians 2:9–11; Revelation 12:11.
15. *The God Catchers*, adapted from a sentence on p. 122.
16. Matthew 5:3–6.

Week Nine

1. See Proverbs 29:25.
2. Noah was five hundred years old when his sons were born (Gen. 5:32), and six hundred years old when the great flood covered the earth (Gen. 7:6).
3. Daniel 9:23.
4. The boundaries are set according to the mercy of your faithful God "who will not allow you to be tempted beyond what you are able, but with the temptation will also make the way of escape, that you may be able to bear it" (1 Cor. 10:13).
5. See Revelation 13:8.
6. For more details about Moses' 1,500-year chase for God's face, see *The God Chasers*, Chapter 10: "Moses' 1,500-Year Pursuit of God's Glory," pp. 139–52.
7. Ibid., p. 139.
8. 1 Samuel 3:19 (italics mine).
9. *Strong's Concordance*, Samuel (Hebrew, #8050).
10. See 1 Samuel 1:9–20.
11. See John 3:16.
12. Matthew 7:11.
13. Compare John 3:16 with Hebrews 12:2 and allow these *true* statements about God and the sacrificial love Jesus demonstrated for us on the cross to "remodel" your thinking about prayer and your relationship with the Deity.
14. See John 15:7; James 4:2–3.
15. According to *Strong's Concordance*, the words *pray* and *prayer* appear in the New Testament

eighty-four times. Just one example of an apostolic command to pray appears in Philippians 4:6–7: "Be anxious for nothing, but in everything by prayer and supplication, with thanksgiving, let your requests be made known to God; and the peace of God, which surpasses all understanding, will guard your hearts and minds through Christ Jesus."

Week Ten

1. Matthew 22:37.
2. 1 Corinthians 8:1.
3. "Nietzsche, Friedrich Wilhelm," Microsoft® Encarta® Online Encyclopedia 2001, 19 June 2001, <www.encarta.msn.com>.
4. 1 Samuel 16:7.
5. See Luke 18:1–5.
6. See 1 Samuel 1.
7. See Luke 22:40–44.
8. See John 3:16.
9. See Acts 3:19.
10. See Genesis 17:19, 21–22; 21:1–7.
11. See Genesis 25:21–26.
12. See Judges 13.
13. See 1 Samuel 1:9–20.
14. See Luke 1:5–25.
15. See Luke 1:26–2:5.
16. See Acts 9:1–11.

Week Eleven

1. As noted on p. 206 in *The God Catchers*: "Let me make it clear that being a 'spiritual traveler in transit' does *not* mean we do not have a fixed local church home. Part of 'chasing God' includes submitting to His Word, the work of the Holy Spirit, and the authority of church leaders ordained and anointed by God to equip us for the work of the ministry. God does more than work with individual believers—most of the New Testament Epistles and the book of Revelation were addressed to churches, not to individuals. *For the record*: Chase God, worship Him in unity with other saints in a local congregation of believers, submit to the spiritual leaders God places over you, and walk in unity. That is the surest path to offering an acceptable sacrifice of praise to Him with your life."
2. See Psalm 51:17.
3. See 2 Corinthians 7:10.
4. See 2 Corinthians 3:18.
5. The Bible mentions these functions of church life many times, including the passages in Hebrews 10:24–25 and Ephesians 4:11–13.
6. See Psalm 34:18.
7. See Exodus 2:11–15.
8. See Numbers 20:7–12.
9. See Matthew 17:1–5.

10. Philippians 4:11–12 (italics mine).

11. 1 Corinthians 9:24, 27 (italics mine).

12. This passage refers to Jesus (Mark 6:3), Peter (Matt. 4:18; Acts 2:14–41), Stephen (Acts 6:1–8), and Paul (Acts 13:46–48; 22:21; 26:4–6). Paul, the self-described Pharisee of Pharisees, became the apostle of the Gentiles and authored many New Testament books or letters to the churches.

13. Paul described the "prize" in 1 Corinthians 9:24–27.

14. See Acts 16:26.

15. See Genesis 8:22; Luke 6:38; 2 Corinthians 9:6.

16. Matthew 5:6, author's paraphrase.

17. Matthew 22:37, author's paraphrase.

18. See Isaiah 55:6.

19. See Acts 16:22–33.

20. Revelation 2:4–5 (italics mine).

21. Exodus 20:5–6.

Week Twelve

1. Philippians 3:13–14 KJV.

2. John 3:30.

3. Matthew 10:16.

4. Corinthians 6:18.

5. See Romans 7:6.

6. See Acts 2:1–6.

7. Acts 2:7–13.

8. Acts 2:14–47.

9. See 1 Peter 2:7–8.

10. 2 Corinthians 12:10. See also 1 Corinthians 2:3–5; 2 Corinthians 12:9.

11. 1 Corinthians 1:26–29.

12. See John 4:6–9.

13. See Romans 2:11; Ephesians 6:9; Colossians 3:25; 1 Peter 1:17.

14. James 2:1, 9.

15. See 2 Timothy 3:5.

16. Please understand that I am *not* urging you or anyone else to disturb a church service or worship gathering. Under the new covenant, and especially in the environment of personal freedom enjoyed in many nations across the globe, we can afford to seek His face freely while doing everything decently and orderly and in respect of those in authority. Talk respectfully with your pastor or the elders of the church. If you can find no freedom to pursue God's presence despite repeated attempts to live at peace with all men, then perhaps you should make sure your heart is clear of resentment and unforgiveness and graciously seek a new church home.

OTHER BOOKS BY TOMMY TENNEY

The God Chasers

God's Favorite House

The God Catchers

The God Catchers Workbook

The Daily Chase (Devotional)

God's Dream Team

God's Secret to Greatness (with David Cape)

Secret Sources of Power (with T. F. Tenney)

About the Author

Tommy Tenney is the author of the best-sellers *The God Chasers*, *God's Favorite House,* and the most recent, *The God Catchers.* With three generations of ministry in his family heritage, Tommy has spent ten years pastoring and over seventeen years in itinerant ministry, traveling to more than thirty nations and extensively throughout the United States. Tommy is a well-known "revivalist" and has been used to spark fires of revival around the world. Tommy has a unique gifting to lead hungry people into the presence of God. He and his wife, Jeannie, understand the value of intimacy and humility in serving God's people. The two central themes of Tommy's GodChasers.network are *unity for the body of Christ* and *pursuing the presence of God.* Tommy and Jeannie reside in Louisiana with their three daughters.

GODChasers.network

GodChasers.network is the ministry of Tommy and Jeannie Tenney. Their heart's desire is to see the presence and power of God fall—not just in churches, but on cities and communities all over the world.

How to contact us:

By Mail:

GodChasers.network
P.O. Box 3355
Pineville, Louisiana 71361
USA

By Phone:

Voice:	318.44CHASE (318.442.4273)
Fax:	318.442.6884
Orders:	888.433.3355

By Internet:

E-mail:	GodChaser@GodChasers.net
Website:	www.GodChasers.net

 *Join Today*

When you join the **GodChasers.network** we'll send you a free teaching tape!

If you share in our vision and want to stay current on how the Lord is using GodChasers.network, please add your name to our mailing list. We'd like to keep you updated on what the Spirit is saying through Tommy. We'll also send schedule updates and make you aware of new resources as they become available.

Sign up by calling or writing to:

Tommy Tenney
GodChasers.network
P.O. Box 3355
Pineville, Louisiana 71361-3355
USA

318-44CHASE (318.442.4273)
or sign up online at http://www.GodChasers.net/lists/

We regret that we are only able to send regular postal mailings to US residents at this time. If you live outside the US you can still add your postal address to our mailing list—you will automatically begin to receive our mailings as soon as they are available in your area.

E-mail Announcement List

If you'd like to receive information from us via e-mail, just provide an e-mail address when you contact us and let us know that you want to be included on the e-mail announcement list!

Run With Us!

Become a GodChasers.network Monthly Revival Partner

Two men, a farmer and his friend, were looking out over the farmer's fields one afternoon. It was a beautiful sight—it was nearly harvest time, and the wheat was swaying gently in the wind. Inspired by this idyllic scene, the friend said, "Look at God's provision!" The farmer replied, "You should have seen it when God had it by Himself!"

This humorous story illustrates a serious truth. Every good and perfect gift comes from Him: but we are supposed to be more than just passive recipients of His grace and blessings. We must never forget that only God can cause a plant to grow—but it is equally important to remember that *we are called to do our part in the sowing, watering, and harvesting.*

When you sow seed into this ministry, you help us reach people and places you could never imagine. The faithful support of individuals like you allows us to send resources, free of charge, to many who would otherwise be unable to obtain them. Your gifts help us carry the Gospel all over the world—including countries that have been closed to evangelism. Would you prayerfully consider partnering with us? As a small token of our gratitude, our Revival Partners who send a monthly gift of $20 or more receive a teaching tape every month. This ministry could not survive without the faithful support of partners like you!

Stand with me now—so we can run together later!

In Pursuit,

Tommy Tenney

Tommy Tenney
& The GodChasers.network Staff

Become a Monthly Revival Partner by calling or writing to:

Tommy Tenney/GodChasers.network
P.O. Box 3355
Pineville, Louisiana 71361-3355
318.44CHASE (318.442.4273)

AUDIOTAPE ALBUMS BY

Tommy Tenney

NEW!
WHAT'S THE FIGHT ABOUT?
(audiotape album) $20 plus $4.50 S&H

Tape 1 — Preserving the Family: God special gift to the world is the family! If we dont preserve the family, the church is one generation from extinction. Gods desire is to heal the wounds of the family from the inside out.

Tape 2 — Unity in the body: An examination of the levels of unity that must be respected and achieved before "Father let them be one" becomes an answered prayer!

Tape 3 — "IF you're throwing dirt, you're just loosing ground!" In "Whats the fight about?" Tommy invades our backyards to help us discover our differences are not so different after all!

FANNING THE FLAMES
(audiotape album) $20 plus $4.50 S&H

Tape 1 — The Application of the Blood and the Ark of the Covenant: Most of the churches in America today dwell in an outer-court experience. Jesus made atonement with His own blood, once for all, and the veil in the temple was rent from top to bottom.

Tape 2 — A Tale of Two Cities—Nazareth & Nineveh: What city is more likely to experience revival: Nazareth or Nineveh? You might be surprised....

Tape 3 — The "I" Factor: Examine the difference between *ikabod* and *kabod* ("glory"). The arm of flesh cannot achieve what needs to be done. God doesn't need us; we need Him.

KEYS TO LIVING THE REVIVED LIFE
(audiotape album) $20 plus $4.50 S&H

Tape 1 — Fear Not: To have no fear is to have faith, and that perfect love casts out fear, so we establish the trust of a child in our loving Father.

Tape 2 — Hanging in There: Have you ever been tempted to give up, quit, and throw in the towel? This message is a word of encouragement for you.

Tape 3 — Fire of God: Fire purges the sewer of our souls and destroys the hidden things that would cause disease. Learn the way out of a repetitive cycle of seasonal times of failure.

VIDEOTAPE ALBUMS BY

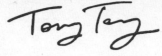

LET'S BUILD A BONFIRE VOL. 1: "LET IT FALL!"

Video $20.00 plus $4.50 S&H

One hour of the best worship and word from the God Chaser gatherings.

CAPTURED IN HIS PRESENCE

Video $25.00 plus $4.50 S&H

An encounter with God captured on tape! (As seen on This is your day with Benny Hinn)

FOLLOW THE MAN ON THE COLT

Video $20.00 plus $4.50 S&H

Are you too proud to ride with Him? Humility is the catalyst that will move your answers from a crawl to a walk to a run to a ride!

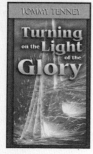

TURNING ON THE LIGHT OF THE GLORY

(video) $20 plus $4.50 S&H

Tommy deals with turning on the light of the glory and presence of God, and he walks us through the necessary process and ingredients to potentially unleash what His Body has always dreamed of.